TESTIMONIALS

"Without Jimmy Walker, there would be no Muhammad Ali Parkinson Center. I can't thank Jimmy enough for all he has done for the MAPC patients."

— Lonnie Ali, wife of Muhammad Ali

"Jimmy Walker is a rare individual. People like him who wish to do good, help others, and generally make the world a better place, asking nothing for themselves, do not come along very often. Helping others less fortunate than ourselves is perhaps the highest calling any of us can hope to achieve. Jimmy is a role model for all."

— Phil Anschutz, investor and Forbes 400 businessman

"Jimmy Walker is a true servant leader! He has few, if any, ego needs. His focus is always on helping others. What a special human being."

— Ken Blanchard, coauthor of *The One Minute Manager*

"There are seven billion people in the world and Jimmy probably knows half of them."

— Dale Brown, former LSU coach and member of College Basketball Hall of Fame

"Jimmy is one of my closest friends. He is important to so many different people. For example, Jimmy started a program for children from the inner city called Bicycles for Kids. That program has given away 10,000 bicycles to kids in needs. He brings in speakers to encourage the homeless in a program at St. Vincent de Paul called Never Give Up."

— Jerry Colangelo, former owner of the Phoenix Suns and Arizona Diamondbacks and managing director of Team USA Basketball

"When I first met Jimmy, I had never sold one record. No one knew who I was. And this dude was so warm and loving and sweet with me. He had so much time for me. I have met so many people in my life, but very few have had the impact of Jimmy Walker."

— Michael Bublé, Grammy award-
winning singer and songwriter

"Jimmy is the gentlest arm-twister I've ever met. And I mean that with the utmost respect. It seems as though Jimmy is asking, but he is really a giver."

— Kevin Costner, Academy Award-
winning actor, director, and producer

"Jimmy is amazing. Right after I bought the Mavericks, I traveled with the team to Phoenix. I didn't know Jimmy, but he approached me at our hotel, introduced himself, and made a simple offer to me. He said, 'Mark, whatever you need, just let me know.' It's a statement I have heard more times than I can count. Coming from most people, it's a throwaway statement. Coming from Jimmy Walker, it's a commitment. And he has always been there for anything I need. Jimmy is a true gentleman with a heart of gold."

— Mark Cuban, Forbes 400 businessman, owner
of the Dallas Mavericks, and star of *Shark Tank*

"Jimmy Walker has mastered the art of relationship maintenance. His ability to make connections and stay involved with people he meets teaches everyone that paying attention to details will go a long way."

— Mike D'Antoni, two-time NBA Coach of the Year

"Jimmy Walker has done a tremendous job putting together Celebrity Fight Night charity events year in and year out."

— Larry Fitzgerald, NFL star for the Arizona Cardinals

"Jimmy is a unique individual. When the bank asks me to list my assets, I start with my friendship with Jimmy. I have so much respect for him as a person, father, and husband."

— **Lou Holtz, former University of Notre Dame head football coach**

"There has not been a year since 2008 when I haven't heard from Jimmy, always gracious, always solicitous, always thoughtful. He's indeed the quintessential gentleman in a modern age when there are so few who can similarly qualify for the description."

— **Clive Davis, Hall of Fame music legend**

"I could not imagine my life without Jimmy Walker in it. He has brought so much joy to me and my family and his dedication to Celebrity Fight Night will never be equaled by anyone else in my lifetime for any other cause . . . period! The mold was definitely broken after God made this man. He is one of a kind, a superhuman, a beautiful friend. He is a gentleman and a gentle man. I'm proud to call him a friend."

— **David Foster, sixteen-time Grammy award-winning musician**

"Jimmy stays in touch with people better than anyone I know. He probably invented Twitter without taking credit for the idea."

— **David Falk, sports agent who represented Michael Jordan**

"Jimmy makes me smile . . . every time . . . all the time. Why? Because he loves and lifts me . . . every time . . . all the time. People don't care how much you know until they know how much you care. Nobody cares like Jimmy!"

— **John Maxwell, bestselling author and professional speaker**

"Jimmy Walker is an outstanding businessman and a go-getter in everything he sets out to accomplish."

— Dan Gilbert, Forbes 400 businessman, founder of
Quicken Loans, and owner of the Cleveland Cavaliers

"Jimmy Walker is one of a kind, a true giver, selfless, full of energy, always looking to uplift other people and make the world a better place. I am proud to know him and grateful for all the incredible good he has done in the world."

— Wyc Grousbeck, owner of the Boston Celtics

"Jimmy is very easy to be around. He is like a beacon of energy. He's grateful for life and always does his best to do the right thing. He's a good family man. I'm absolutely amazed at the people he meets and the relationships he builds. In Phoenix, he gives you his car, he gives you his home, and he gives you his office."

— Reggie Jackson, Major League Baseball
Hall of Famer, known as "Mr. October"

"Every single year when I played for the Chicago Bulls, Jimmy always had a car waiting for me when I arrived in Phoenix to play the Suns, which was a generous act of kindness I always appreciated."

— Michael Jordan, former NBA superstar

"I call Jimmy the Big Contact."

— Shaquille O'Neal, four-time NBA
champion and Hall of Fame center

"Jimmy is a giving guy who cares about people. We need more Jimmy Walkers out there giving back."

— Dick Vitale, college basketball analyst

"Jimmy Walker is a good man. He is very passionate."

— **Carrie Underwood, country music superstar**

"There are a few people in the world like Jimmy Walker who wants to help every person he's ever met. But the secret is he expects nothing in return."

— **Harvey Mackay, bestselling author
and professional speaker**

"Jimmy is a great networker. He calls you if you have a good game or if you're going through tough times. That's a big part of his business success. He shows he cares and is thinking about you."

— **Steve Nash, head coach of the Brooklyn
Nets and two-time MVP**

"Jimmy Walker's legacy is not only the thousands of individuals he has enabled and empowered. His true legacy is in the model of a purpose driven life, the secret of happiness. Relationships are the oxygen of success."

— **Marilyn Nelson, former CEO of Carlson**

"Jimmy is the master of relationships. He understands that personal relationships are more important in business than spreadsheets analysis. He has a unique combination of personal drive, energy, and kindness that works for him and allows him to help many others."

— **Doug Parker, American Airlines CEO.**

"Jimmy has mastered the art of smothering you with kindness, an omnipresent friendly face. He is totally sincere. He's simply the nicest guy in the world."

— **Walter Scott Jr., Forbes 400 businessman**

"It seems almost anytime something significant happens, I get a note from Jimmy or a phone call. He is better than anybody I know at staying in touch. There's not a single person I've ever met in Phoenix who doesn't like Jimmy Walker."

— **Jerry Reinsdorf, Forbes 400 businessman and owner of the Chicago Bulls and Chicago White Sox**

"Meeting Jimmy for the first time was like meeting the Energizer Bunny. God's messenger on steroids. How can one man have so many projects on his plate and still have time for his own private life? The answer: passion."

— **Lionel Richie, Grammy award-winning singer, songwriter, producer, and actor**

"Jimmy is a great friend. If I could hire him as one of my assistant coaches, I wouldn't hesitate. Because coaching is about motivating people. He's a coach of people. He has the ability to bring people together from all walks of life. He is a champion."

— **Doc Rivers, head coach of the Philadelphia 76ers**

"Staying in contact with people like Jimmy makes you feel connected. It is like creating your own network of people. Jimmy is well connected."

— **Emmitt Smith, Hall of Fame NFL star with the Dallas Cowboys**

"Jimmy is one of those inspirational human beings who makes everybody he comes in contact with happier about their own situation. Jimmy is one of those selfless saints. He is the ultimate team player."

— **Bill Walton, hall of fame NBA player and broadcaster**

"Jimmy Walker has more true friends than anyone I have ever known. I know for a fact Jimmy would do anything I ask of him. Just as he knows I would do anything he asks of me. There are only a few people in my life who fall into this category. He is a 'FRIEND.' Jimmy is a very special man with a mission, designed above all else, to help others."

— Kenny Rogers, the late country music superstar

"Few people I know understand the priority and value of relationships as well as my friend Jimmy Walker. I highly recommend this book."

— Rick Warren, author of *The Purpose Driven Life*

"If anyone knows the value of creating and maintaining honest relationships, it's Jimmy Walker. With Jimmy, it's not just a two-way street. He is always willing to give more to you, or to a good cause, than he ever asks in return."

— Bob Costas, Emmy award-winning sportscaster

"To see how Jimmy Walker can connect to people is one of the greatest things I've seen. You know at once he's sincere. He has that feel about him. Some people you know you are leery about . . . you know, *what's your angle?* But Jimmy is so pure. I'm blown away by him."

— Reba McEntire, award-winning country
music artist, songwriter, and actress

IT'S ALL ABOUT
RELATIONSHIPS

Building a Life that Matters

JIMMY WALKER

Forefront
BOOKS

Published by Forefront Books.

Cover Design by Bruce Gore, Gore Studio Inc.
Interior Design by Bill Kersey, Kersey Graphics

ISBN: 978-1-63763-037-2
ISBN: 978-1-63763-038-9 (e-Book)

This book is dedicated to the most important people in my life ... my wife, Nancy, who is my best friend and has shaped my heart ... my daughters, Laurie and Jennifer ... my grandchildren, Jack, Max, Macy, Jonathan, Justin, Mabel, Kennedy ... my late daughter, Cynthia Faye ... and my late son, Scott, whom God used to change my priorities.

CONTENTS

FOREWORD

OVER THE YEARS, I HAVE ALWAYS MADE IT A POINT NOT TO BE friends with people who sell life insurance.

I don't want to be playing cards, say, and have that friend suddenly ask if my kids were protected if I suddenly died before I won the next hand.

Jimmy Walker was the exception. We met at a Clippers basketball game, the perfect place to discuss death, but he was very genuine, talking eagerly about point guards and estate planning, and after I checked him out with several big-name athletes that he worked with, I agreed to talk with him. He is a sweet man, kind and generous, talks a mile a minute, but he has a great heart that is as big as the Valley he lives in in Arizona.

Jimmy is that rare person who just wants to do good. His devotion to Muhammad Ali and to the Parkinson's research center in Phoenix was inspiring to say the least. Over the years, he was the driving force for Fight Night, a fantastic evening that brought sports heroes and show business entertainers together to raise incredible sums of money for charity. I have been part of this event many times, and it never failed to be one of the great, fun, inspirational, and emotional evenings of the year. However, what was a one-nighter for me was just one of many events that Jimmy was a part of over the course of a year.

Jimmy Walker never asks for more than you can give him, but you always want to give him something more because you know that it's going to a good cause. Someone tragically ill, a family dealing with a loved one's illness, a homeless shelter, a hospital . . . those are among the ones that have been touched by his relentless pursuit of helping those in need.

This book may be about personal relationships, but Jimmy has a bigger relationship with the world. A world in need that he only wants to help. Selfless souls like Jimmy are hard to come by. I value our friendship, and to this day we have never played cards together.

Billy Crystal

INTRODUCTION

I AM NOT A CELEBRITY, ALTHOUGH I HAVE MANY FAMOUS FRIENDS. I am not a scholar, although I have learned a great deal during my journey. I'm a regular guy who has seen some of my dreams come true.

I have spent nearly six decades building relationships. I have learned that, in life, you need focus, passion, and mental toughness.

I'm writing this book because I want my experience with relationships to help other people, not because I want people to think more highly of me. I want people to learn from my good fortune and the mistakes I have made.

Throughout this book, I may refer to scriptures in the Bible and the importance of my faith. If this is not of value to you, please, rest assured I will not try to force my faith on you.

I'm also writing this book in memory of my son, Scott, who passed away from an accidental overdose at age forty-three. Just three days before his passing, Scott said, "Dad, I want to build a sober living home to help other people suffering from the same disease I have."

I replied, "Scott, your dad will help you build this sober living home."

All of the profits from this book will be donated to our nonprofit Christian-based sober living homes in Phoenix and Scottsdale. Our family is dedicated to helping others who are suffering from this terrible disease.

CHAPTER 1

HI, I'M JIMMY!

Don't Be Afraid to Ask

I GREW UP IN CARTHAGE, ILLINOIS, A SMALL MIDWESTERN town of about 3,000 people. We never locked our front door.

Nobody had security alarms. You trusted people. You could get ahold of anybody because everyone's number was listed.

It didn't take me long to start working the phones.

At age seven, my father drove 150 miles to Busch Stadium in Missouri. We went to see one of my heroes, Stan Musial, play for the St. Louis Cardinals. After the game, we even went to the restaurant that Musial owned, a steakhouse called Stan Musial and Biggie's. I remember ordering a Yogi Berra hamburger.

Upon leaving, I picked up a book of matches for a souvenir. On the way home, I realized an address and phone number were on the inside cover of the matchbook. I knew exactly what I had to do.

I called the restaurant the very next day.

"This is Jimmy Walker in Carthage and Stan the Man wants to speak to me!" I said into the phone.

It worked. My unique approach effectively cleared the air. And it still works today.

I told Musial he was my favorite player. He asked how I was doing in baseball. I called him back several times and Musial always took time to visit with a seven-year-old boy he didn't know, the one who kept calling him from Carthage, Illinois.

I told my family and friends about the conversations with Musial, but nobody believed me. They thought I was exaggerating. But I was only getting started.

When we'd travel as a family, we would occasionally go through Commerce, Oklahoma, which was the home of Yankees star Mickey Mantle. I would get his number from the telephone information service. And I would always try to call him collect.

Mrs. Mantle would always pick up and say, "Sorry, we don't accept collect calls." But I was undeterred. I wanted to speak with Mickey Mantle, and I've never had a fear about calling people.

Growing up in the 1950s, I did the usual things. The ice cream truck came around our neighborhood with music blaring, and I thought that was the greatest job in the world. I loved the attention the ice cream man received. He seemed very important to me. Everybody ran to him when he showed up, and I thought that was really cool. I wanted to drive an ice cream truck.

I had a pet burro, a small donkey given to me by a family friend, Paul Dennis. I named her Juanita after my sixth-grade teacher. The burro lived in our backyard and would follow me all the way to school. Every time, the teacher would politely ask me to take Juanita home.

Firecrackers were also a big deal in my hometown, and they were legal in nearby Missouri. I would get on my bicycle and ride through Keokuk, Iowa, and cross into Missouri, just to get those firecrackers. Back in those days, it was no big deal for an eight-year-old to ride his

Me and Juanita

bike down an interstate highway, crossing through two states along the way.

Carthage was a typical Midwestern city. It had a town square with a courthouse in the center. We had the Woodbine movie theater, where I often found my brother Jonnie holding hands with two different girls at the same time, one on each side of him. I sensed this was not normal. I held him hostage. I made him pay me a dime not to tell all parents involved. My business instincts were razor sharp at a very young age. After the movies, my friends and I would hang out in the square. The farmers would come out and sit on benches. We could gossip with the best of them.

Carthage also has an infamous jail where Mormon founders Joseph and Hyrum Smith were murdered by a town mob while awaiting trial in 1844. A lot of my Mormon friends have visited Carthage on a religious pilgrimage. In high school, I would bring up my hometown to Mormon girls and wonder why I couldn't get a second date.

The townspeople were also very protective. If you saw somebody in the Carthage town square that you didn't recognize, everyone would stare at him. Who is that person? That was common in small towns, where everyone knows everybody and it's easy to spot a stranger.

But our parents trusted us. Maybe too much.

One time, my older brother Jonnie put a tin can on my head. He took a BB gun and started shooting holes through the tin can. Eventually, the mailman had to have a talk with my mom. He told her, "You better stop this or they could make young Jimmy blind."

In 1953, my dad had the first air-conditioned car in Carthage. It was an Oldsmobile, with big pipes in the back. In the wintertime, we would get about eight of our friends and attach sleds to the bumper of the car. My dad would drive us down the icy roads in Carthage. We had a blast. If that happened today, police would put my dad in jail for something so dangerous.

Other times, we would get in the backs of pickup trucks and drive to the Mississippi River, where we would jump in and swim. Nobody does that today, even though the river was probably as polluted then as it is now. But nobody cared. Nobody died. We didn't wear seat belts. It was just a different era.

My dad also had the first color television set in Carthage. And you know what it was? He had some colored cellophane that he taped on the corner. And we called it a color television. That's how we lived.

You know what else I remember? Popcorn.

Popcorn was a very big deal in our house. Just like former President Ronald Reagan, my dad believed that all great things begin in the kitchen. Dad would have the real-deal popcorn kernels sent in from Iowa. He would not fool around with anything fancy or electronic. He bought the best sweet cream butter he could find. He referred to margarine as "phony butter."

He would make that popcorn in a pan over a fire, rocking it hard on the burner. And every day at 5:00 p.m., seven days a week, he would make popcorn for our family and friends. Sometimes, there'd be as many as ten people gathered in our kitchen, eating from two large bowls.

Former Lakers great Magic Johnson once said he was always ready to play when he could smell the popcorn inside the Forum. Our popcorn was so good, you could smell it in another neighborhood. I can still taste it to this very day.

If there was anything unusual about my Midwestern childhood, it was my passion for sports and athletes. It consumed me.

We played basketball and baseball all the time. We never stopped. We played at night under the streetlights. We played when the weather was freezing. My mom would always wonder what happened to all the salt in her kitchen. Well, my brothers and I needed that salt to clear off frozen basketball courts.

By the time I was seven, I had two role models: Jackie Robinson of the Brooklyn Dodgers and Goose Tatum of the Harlem Globetrotters. They were both winners, and I wanted to be just like them. I wanted to hit a baseball like Jackie and handle a basketball like Goose. Nothing was going to stop me.

Academically, it wasn't like I wanted to study hard and go to Harvard. It was all about sports. If I could rewind the clock, I would be studying a lot more and playing less basketball. But I had no interest.

I was also raised by parents who never said no.

My father, Claire, was an insurance salesman, a people person, a real character. Dad was also a giver. He was extremely generous. An outgoing personality. Dad would do anything for us. Dad would drive us anywhere.

Dad was also very impatient. One summer, we took a trip from Carthage to Phoenix, Arizona, then north to Wyoming. We went through the Grand Canyon and Yellowstone—the site of

Old Faithful—at warp speed, as if they were drive-thru restaurants. Incredibly, we completed that trip in six days. Dad always seemed to be in a hurry.

We took our terrier, Fluffy, with us. Aside from a very poor personality and a bad attitude, Fluffy also had a gas problem. It was bad. He smelled the whole way to Arizona. He was cutting gas constantly. Meanwhile, my parents were smoking cigarettes in the front seat. That was not a pleasant experience, but, as kids, you learn to adjust.

We kept thinking Fluffy's gas would come to an end at some point. We got through Tulsa, through Wichita, and into New Mexico, but Fluffy wouldn't stop farting. Dad said, "To hell with Fluffy, we're going to leave him here. I can't take this smell anymore! Someone is going to take care of him here in New Mexico."

Mom put her foot down and said, "He is not staying in New Mexico! He is going with us." She was ready to divorce him over that. Fluffy climbed back in the car and off we went.

My brothers and I were only four years apart, so road trips generally included backseat fighting. Dad always countered with old-school strategy. He would take the back of his hand and start swinging blindly while he was driving. If you were in the area, you caught one across the face.

"But, Dad, I didn't start it!" I would say.

"I don't know who in the Sam Hell started it, but I know I got the right one," Dad would respond.

On our trip to Arizona, I got into an argument with my brothers near the Grand Canyon, and when we got there, Dad took his hand and pushed my head down as punishment. So I never saw the Grand Canyon on that trip. And I grew up with loving parents. That's just how we were raised at the time.

We went on to Wyoming to see Old Faithful at Yellowstone and we learned the geyser went off every sixty minutes. Except we got there thirty minutes early, and that was a problem. My dad said, "To hell with it. Let's go." We never did see it. My dad bought a postcard instead. He thought that was good enough. And that's all we saw of Old Faithful.

I still haven't seen Old Faithful erupt.

Dad was always on the go. On long road trips, whenever we had to use the bathroom, my brothers and I would have to pee in a Coke or Pepsi bottle and throw it out the window. My dad wouldn't stop the car. There was always someplace we had to be. We always had to make time. That's just how we rolled.

Dad was a general agent with a life insurance company. He had six agents working for him. One of them ran into a cash flow problem.

He asked my dad for a $3,000 loan.

"No problem," my dad said, pulling out his checkbook.

Several days later, the agent nervously approached my dad.

My mom made me wear that bowtie.

Introducing myself to All-American Carl Cain
at a basketball game in Iowa City.

"Mr. Walker, the bank called me," he said. "The check you wrote for $3,000 actually bounced."

Dad's response?

"Well, Jim, that shows you how much I love you! I wrote you a check for money I didn't even have," he said.

My dad also would swear a lot, frequently using the Lord's name in vain. Many years later, as a young adult, I told my dad that "dammit" was not God's last name. I never heard him swear again.

But we were a very close family. And I learned from my father how important it was to be honest along with having a good attitude and being enthusiastic. I fed off the energy of my dad and two older brothers.

My mother, Pearl, always told us she didn't want us talking about sports or life insurance at the dinner table. Nevertheless, when we sat down as a family, the conversation always wound up centering on those very two things: sports and life insurance. My mom just smiled, laughed, and listened.

My mom also had the best collection of handkerchiefs in Carthage. I saw to that.

At age six, I earned a $1 allowance that I would pick up every week at my dad's office. And then I'd go next door to the Ben Franklin five-and-dime store and buy my mom a handkerchief that cost ten cents. I must've bought one hundred for her. And every time I gave her one, she acted like it was exactly what she needed.

My dad frequently drove us to Iowa City to watch the University of Iowa's basketball team in the 1950s. I could barely stay in my seat. I was enchanted by live professional sporting events. I wanted more access. I wanted to be in the heart of the action.

My brother Gary once gave me a hat with a card in the front that read, "Press." It was a joke, but I wore it to all the games. And I didn't consider it a joke at all, not with the magic powers it seemed to provide.

Nowadays, an eight-year-old "journalist" wouldn't stand a chance of gaining special access in modern arenas. But that makeshift "Press" hat allowed me to sit on the floor and take pictures of the players with my $6 Kodak Brownie Hawkeye camera. I acted like I knew what I was doing. I was not afraid to take the big chance. The ushers saw me and said, "Let the kid sit there."

This is how I met the father of Bill Seaberg in 1955, whose son was a starting guard on Iowa's basketball team. I asked Mr. Seaberg if I could go in the locker room and meet the team. He said, "Of course."

I went inside the locker room with my camera and started taking pictures. I thought nothing of the fact that most of the players were half-naked and were quickly covering themselves up with towels. I honestly thought they wanted to see me.

Carthage College also had a basketball team in our hometown. At halftime, I would go out on the floor in my socks and start shooting baskets, putting on a display for everyone. Nobody else did that because they knew they weren't supposed to be on the floor at halftime. But I'd just go out there at six and seven years old, dribble behind my back, and shoot hook shots, showing off a little bit but just having fun. And the crowd always encouraged me to do it. That was just kind of who I was at the time.

I couldn't have cared less about school. I just wanted to play basketball and baseball. I just wanted to meet pro athletes. I would wear my "Press" hat at all the games and no one ever removed me. They just let me do my thing. Today I couldn't go anywhere like that. But in those days, everybody trusted everybody.

Meanwhile, my improbable phone conversations with Musial only emboldened me to make more connections.

I began writing letters. Tons of them. I'd write ten to fifteen letters a day to professional baseball and basketball players requesting autographed pictures. I had a winning strategy: I told everyone they were my favorite player. I told some of them that my mother wanted to marry them. I had my mom marrying about ten different guys.

One of them even wrote back saying, "I hope you feel better."

Bottom line: I said whatever it took to get an autographed picture. I completely rejected the idea of rejection.

I must have received 300–400 responses from players like Mickey Mantle, Yogi Berra, Goose Tatum, Stan Musial, Duke Snider, Bob Cousy, George Mikan, Elroy Hirsch, and Otto Graham. As a young kid, I could not wait to go to the mailbox. I would get two to three responses every day.

Satchel Paige was one of the best pitchers in Major League Baseball. His fastball was clocked at 98.6 miles per hour, which was unheard of in his generation. He answered my letter on August 13, 1953. Back then, postage stamps cost two cents. Can you believe

Satchel wanted me to reimburse him next time I wanted a picture? For two cents!

I had my own crew in Carthage consisting of five friends whom I met in 1949 while in the first grade: Joe Dion, Terry Newell, Randy Reu, Jerry Aten, and Davey Larson. We've remained extremely close over the years, although Randy and Jerry have since passed. And they also began writing letters to professional athletes.

Racing to the mailbox became a competition between me and my friends. But I was way ahead of them. I was writing way more than they were, a trait I would carry throughout my adult life.

Leroy Robert "Satchel" Paige, pitcher for the St. Louis Browns

In one of my many mistakes, I didn't save the majority of the autographed pictures and letters I received. I still have about a dozen, but hundreds of them are missing, including personal notes from Mickey Mantle and Stan Musial. Somehow, they got lost over the years.

But the lessons remain.

Even as a kid, I always felt if you don't ask, you don't get. Disappointment is inevitable. I learned early the worst answer I can get by asking is no.

I possessed the idea that I was going to get inside the locker room, sit on the floor, and nothing was going to stop me. I talked my way in and faked the rest. Most of the ushers ignored me. I moved on implied consent and they rarely stopped me. If they started to object, I moved to another part of the gym and usually got what I wanted. That was my mentality as a young kid.

Today I have learned considerably more patience and perhaps better judgment than when I was younger. But as a kid, I recognized the barriers that come with fear.

If you label something as fear, it creates false alarms. Many times what you're feeling is more of a concern than fear. And it's much easier to break down a concern than it is to break down a fear. Because fear creates a block that hinders your creative thinking.

I've never shied away from meeting new people. I'm as fired up today as I was back then when it comes to making new connections, whether it's calling Stan Musial or writing Mickey Mantle. I have always enjoyed the pursuit and the challenge.

Fear rarely crosses my mind. I still remember what Babe Ruth once said: "Never let the fear of striking out get in your way." Believe me, I've struck out many times. The trick is being willing to fail.

Even as a youngster, I never felt failure was final. I never thought it was impossible to sit on the floor with adults and take pictures as an eight year old. I expected it. The opposite of fear is faith, and the opposite of faith is doubt. If we confront fear, we can achieve great things.

I have learned that nothing great is ever achieved without enthusiasm and the willingness to take a risk. And I have never stopped asking.

Don't be afraid to ask.

CHAPTER 2

MEETING REG-GIE!

College Days at Arizona State University

WE HEADED WEST IN 1956. DAD MOVED OUR FAMILY TO Phoenix. He spared no expense.

He probably surrendered his entire net worth to buy our family a house with a swimming pool. That was amazing. We came from a small place in the Midwest that didn't have a swimming pool in the entire town.

Then, Dad had a full-sized basketball court built in our backyard. This had two baskets, one positioned on each end of the court. He even installed lights so we could play in the evening. My dad was awesome. So was my mom, who would do anything to help our family.

They knew it was my dream to become a professional basketball player.

My odds were not good. As a freshman at Phoenix Central High School, I was only four foot ten and weighed eighty-five pounds. I had friends tell me I was too small for high school basketball. But nothing could stop me. And I left nothing to chance.

I wore my flattop hairstyle as high as I could grow it, and I would stretch it out with Butch wax just to make the short hairs stand up as high as possible. I would even put on an extra pair of socks, hoping it would add to my height.

For most of my young life, I was the shortest player on my basketball team. I was also the best player. Because nobody practiced more than I did. No one outworked me.

I dribbled a basketball everywhere I went. I dribbled that basketball to school. I dribbled while listening to "Sweet Georgia Brown" over and over again, the song that had been adopted by the Harlem Globetrotters a few years earlier. I dribbled so much I would literally wear out the tread on the ball's surface.

I wore ankle weights to class. I did leg and calf stretches while sitting in my seat while the teacher was lecturing. I squeezed a rubber ball to develop strength in my wrists and my forearms. I was lifting weights when nobody was lifting weights. I was married to basketball at a very young age.

At five foot ten, I could almost dunk a basketball. I set a school record for most points in a game (thirty-six), helping Central High finish third in the state. I was named first team All-State and fielded close to a dozen scholarship offers.

I narrowed my colleges to the University of Oregon and Arizona State University. I visited Eugene but I chose ASU. Even at seventeen, I was visualizing my future. I knew someday I would be in the life insurance business in Phoenix, and I wanted to be making contacts where I'd be making a living.

I also knew this because I had started selling life insurance in high school. I guess I was a natural salesman. It ran in the family. I targeted busboys at restaurants and carry-out clerks at the grocery store, selling them on the benefits of a forced savings program.

The policy I sold most often was $5,000 whole life and $5,000 accidental death that paid double if you were killed in an accident. The premium was $6.78 a month. My first client was a young man, Dave Zimmerman, who worked a job scooping ice cream at 31 Flavors. I had to chase him down at a Bob's Big Boy restaurant to get his premium paid on time.

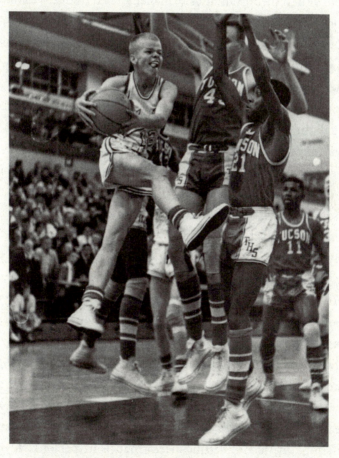

Playing for Central High in 1962 . . . Michael Jordan and I had one thing in common: we both stuck out our tongues when we were driving to the hoop.

He died three weeks later in a car crash in San Luis, Mexico.

I delivered $10,000 to his mom and dad. I was seventeen years old. That amount of money is worth probably $500,000 dollars by today's standards, and that money came from their son. At that moment, I understood what life insurance could do for a family.

I'll never forget another one of my early clients. George was a young busboy I met while eating at a local restaurant. We struck up a conversation, then started discussing insurance in the restaurant's kitchen. When the restaurant's manager kicked us out, we continued our conversation at a nearby drugstore.

George seemed to like my sales pitch. He kept nodding his head, agreeing with everything I said. Like any good salesman, I moved on implied consent.

I took out an application and handed George a pen. I watched with delight as he signed every form. And when the inspection arrived, I received a real surprise:

George was deaf. We could not deliver the policy because he didn't qualify for the insurance.

Moral of the story: I wasn't afraid to ask. Even to someone who couldn't hear a word I was saying.

My efforts paid off in the long run. Whenever I sold a $5,000 policy, I earned a commission of $45. That was good money back in 1962, and I probably sold twenty-five policies to busboys and carry-out clerks in Phoenix. I banked several thousand dollars in the process. I was on my way.

It was a good thing, too, because my basketball career was headed right to the bench.

Arizona State University's head basketball coach, Ned Wulk, had recruited me out of Central High School, having witnessed my thirty-six-point, record-setting performance in person. He would later say that he never had a player who "hustled more than Jimmy Walker."

*I'm sure the NBA scouts were looking in another direction
when I played at Arizona State in 1964 and 1965.*

Truth is, I was a really good high school player who was very
mediocre in college. I lacked confidence when I played. I was the
third guard for a while, and then I became the fourth guard. I hustled,
but they were better ballplayers. I was around guys who were playing
above the rim. It taught me plenty about disappointment.

Jim Whitehead was my best friend on the team. His nickname
was Toots, which was perfect for him. He was the most popular

player in the locker room and a real offensive threat with his accurate jump shot.

There were times when I had to guard Jumpin' Joe Caldwell in practice. That didn't work out well for me. Joe was six foot five and could leap out of the gym. He won a gold medal at the Olympics in 1964, became an NBA All-Star, and was so athletic that the Rams reportedly offered him a football contract. Not sure what coach was thinking there asking me to guard Jumpin' Joe Caldwell, unless he was trying to force my early retirement from basketball.

After every game, my mother always felt like Coach Wulk should've started me. I said, "Mom, if I was better, he would've!"

Watching my basketball dreams evaporate was a painful experience, but I never considered myself a failure because my effort was always 110 percent. I realized that disappointment and adversity were part of growing up. Even though it was the biggest setback I had ever experienced in my life at that time.

But my college life was pretty good. I continued selling life insurance while on a basketball scholarship. I was a member of the Sigma Alpha Epsilon fraternity. I was runner-up as school homecoming king to Sal Bando, a baseball player who would later star for the Oakland Athletics.

I owned a silver convertible Corvette. It cost $10,000, which I paid for out of the money I earned selling insurance policies. I believe I had the first mobile phone on ASU's campus, which was about the size of a suitcase. I had one of the first fax machines on the market, which probably weighed about 200 pounds. At age eighteen, I thought a mobile phone and a fax machine would help me sell more life insurance.

My social program was to pull up to an intersection in my Corvette convertible with the top down, talking on my mobile phone while playing Motown through the car speakers. It was my world and everybody else was just living in it.

In our fraternity house, there was an ongoing competition. Who could date the prettiest girls? Who could take out a ten? I used to take out a lot of tens while I lived at that fraternity. Problem was, sometimes I had to take out two fives to get there.

Either way, I think I may have majored in basketball and minored in girls at ASU. I also became close friends with Reggie Jackson, a baseball player who became so famous they named a candy bar in his honor, a player who once described himself as "the straw that stirred the drink."

I attended ASU on a basketball scholarship. Reggie was there on a football scholarship. During his freshmen year, he walked past the baseball diamond to his dormitory and stopped by and took some swings.

Bobby Winkles, the ASU baseball coach, saw Reggie's immense talent immediately, and the rest is history. It wasn't long before baseball was Reggie's best sport.

I met him at the Devil's Den, a popular hangout in Tempe. We were both cutting a night class. I went up and introduced myself. I said, "Hey, Reggie. I'm on the basketball team. You probably don't know me. But I know you."

I'll never forget his response:

"Jimmy, someday I will be good as Willie Mays or Hank Aaron, and I'll be in the Hall of Fame."

Reggie was seventeen or eighteen at the time. I remember thinking, *This is either the cockiest guy or the most confident guy I've ever met in my life.* But he backed it up. He pursued his dreams and made it happen.

Reggie was also my best friend in college. We hung out. We went to a lot of Phoenix Suns games together. Our favorite player was David Lattin, a center for the Suns who was part of that famous Texas Western team that beat Kentucky for the championship in 1966. His nickname was "Big Daddy," and we could talk about him all day long. Suns great Dick Van Arsdale was also a favorite of ours.

There were a lot of great players coming into ASU at the time. Rick Monday and Sal Bando were both part of the 1965 team that won an NCAA championship. But you could tell right away that Reggie was different.

Reggie would sometimes wash his car three times a day. He ironed his uniform before every baseball game he played. If you ate at his house, you had to clean up right away before you made a mess. He was immaculate.

He hit fifteen home runs in his first season at ASU using a wooden bat. That was a school record. He was named the Sporting News National Player of the Year. He was so good at baseball that he was selected with the second overall pick in baseball's amateur draft in 1967. It didn't take him long to become a household name.

Every agent on the planet wanted to represent Reggie, who was about to sign his first professional contract with the Athletics. I introduced him to my brother, Gary, who got the job.

Gary represented Reggie for all of his baseball contracts. The first one was worth $75,000, and, at the time, a Cadillac Eldorado was the vehicle of choice for most professional athletes. Reggie drove a Pontiac Bonneville for probably five years. He didn't go crazy with cars and clothes. He invested his money in real estate. Reggie was a really good businessman. Still is.

When it came to negotiating Reggie's contracts, Gary would climb into his Winnebago and meet baseball owners at various points in the country. My brother was afraid of flying, although he'd say that it wasn't the flying that bothered him but the falling he found concerning. So he drove. He met Yankees owner George Steinbrenner in Chicago. He did the same with Padres owner Ray Kroc, the McDonald's hamburger tycoon who tried to sign

Reggie and reportedly said to him, "The trouble with you, Reggie, is that you think you're God. But you're wrong. I am."

Early on in Reggie's career, my brother taught him how to talk to the media. Gary taught him how to come into clubhouse after you have gone 0-for-4 with four strikeouts and how to handle yourself when things aren't going well. Reggie credits my brother with all of that. Reggie was a very strong personality. He will tell you what he thinks. Gary was not a yes-man. Gary will get in your face. I think Reggie respected that.

When I attempted to sell Reggie his first life insurance policy, he seemed confused. I told him that it was the perfect time, how he was young and the premiums were as low as they were going to get.

He asked, "Why do I need a $1 million life insurance policy?"

I said, "Reggie, who do you love? Who do you really care about?"

He was probably thinking about his four or five girlfriends. So I handed him a legal pad. I told him to write down the names. He got very quiet.

He wrote down sixteen names of people in his life that he really loved. His mom, dad, brothers, sisters, and a couple of cousins. The last two names were my daughters, Laurie and Jennifer, who were five and three at the time. These were the beneficiaries on his first $1 million policy.

I visited Reggie a lot when he played for the A's, maybe fifteen to twenty times. I stayed at his house in Oakland. I always had access to the clubhouse and the best seats. Reggie introduced me to all his teammates. Better yet, he told them all to buy life insurance from Jimmy Walker. The first one who did was All-Star pitcher Vida Blue.

Reggie became very famous very quickly. At the 1971 All-Star Game in Detroit, he hit a home run that hit a transformer on the roof of Tiger Stadium. Otherwise, it would have completely left the stadium.

He hit three home runs in the 1977 World Series off three different pitchers on three consecutive pitches. He led two different teams to five championships in the span of seven years. His clutch hitting was so good during postseason that they called him Mr. October.

I remember visiting Reggie in Florida during spring training. He was driving a Rolls Royce and reading the sports section of a newspaper at the same time. I said, "You can't be reading that newspaper while you're driving a Rolls!" He didn't think anything of it.

Reggie is also very loyal. He always remembers where he came from, especially with me. He has never changed in that regard and has always treated me the same. He's even taken my kids trick-or-treating on Halloween. He opened a lot of doors for me.

Back in 1973, *Sport* magazine named him Player of the Year. They wanted to honor him in New York, and Reggie invited me as his guest. Our flight to New York was scheduled to leave at 12:30 a.m., and at 11:55 p.m., we were still at Reggie's house. He was talking on the phone to Giants superstar Willie McCovey. I finally interrupted: "Reggie, we have to get going!"

He called TWA headquarters in Kansas City. He said he was Reggie Jackson and asked if they could hold the plane for fifteen minutes. They said they could hold it for him, but only for ten minutes. We drove like maniacs to the airport and barely made our flight. But it was amazing to see the influence Reggie had developed since our early days at ASU.

My kids grew up loving Reggie. In the late 1970s, we went to see the Yankees play the Angels. We were in the lobby of the Disneyland Hotel when I spotted baseball great Joe DiMaggio. I introduced myself to the former Yankees superstar. I told him how much I respected him. As he was thanking me for the kind words, I saw my wife and daughter approaching.

"Nancy, I'd like you to meet Joe DiMaggio," I said.

Then I turned to my daughter.

"Jennifer, this is the greatest baseball player of all time, Joe DiMaggio!" I said.

My daughter was five years old at the time. With pigtails and dimples, she looked up at DiMaggio.

"No he isn't, Daddy!" she said. "You told me Reggie Jackson was the greatest!"

Oops.

CHAPTER 3

WHAT A RACQUET!

Owning a World Team Tennis Franchise

I BECAME A SPORTS OWNER IN 1975. WHAT A CRAZY BUSINESS. Where else can you be named Executive of the Year while losing your shirt?

I partnered with Reggie Jackson and my brother Gary to purchase the Denver Racquets, a charter member and reigning champions of World Team Tennis. It was a mixed-gender, professional tennis league cofounded by the great Billie Jean King. It was built on the premise of gender equity, the only professional sports league where men and women had equal roles in the outcome.

It was a great idea.

The sport was a big deal in Phoenix at the time, and a big deal in this country. We allowed coaches to do their thing during matches. We had multicolored courts. We turned tennis into a social gathering.

I faced stiff competition. One of my fellow owners was Dr. Jerry Buss, who later purchased the Los Angeles Lakers and helped guide that franchise to sixteen NBA Finals appearances in thirty-three seasons, winning ten championship rings. Another was Robert Kraft, who later purchased the New England Patriots, winning six Super Bowl titles and counting.

Elton John even wrote his hit single "Philadelphia Freedom" in honor of cofounder Billie Jean King and his favorite team in the WTT.

As new owner of the Racquets, I made a big splash.

I recruited and signed Chris Evert, the number one female tennis player in the world. I flew to Florida and met with Chris and her father, Jimmy. I signed her to a two-year deal. I paid her $150,000 a year, the highest salary in the WTT.

She was a legitimate superstar. She was revered as the quintessential "girl next door." She was only twenty-one and had already won Wimbledon, the U.S. Open, and the French Open.

To promote our team, I hired Bobby Riggs, the 1941 Wimbledon champion, best known for playing and losing to King in the 1973 Battle of the Sexes.

Bobby was among the most positive people I've ever met. He did a phenomenal job putting on tennis clinics in Phoenix. He was great with our season ticket holders. He attended team parties. He walked around the arena passing out Sugar Daddy® candy pops, shaking hands, and thanking people for coming.

He was not a cheater or a fraud in any way. He was not a con man either. But he was one of the greatest hustlers you've ever met. There's a big difference.

Bobby also enjoyed gambling. He'd bet on anything, anytime. He would come into our office and pitch nickels against our secretaries. The closest coin to the wall would win the pot, and he would often take $4–5 from the ladies in the office.

I'd tell Bobby that he needed to stop taking money from our employees, some of whom really needed that money.

With a smile on his face, he would say, "Jimmy, you know they love to tell their friends they just got hustled by Bobby Riggs!"

There were plenty of times when Bobby begged me to let him coach the Racquets. I stood firm. I told him I couldn't have him betting and taking money from our season ticket holders. They'd run us both out of town.

I lost more than a few dollars to Bobby on the golf course. We often played at La Costa golf course in Carlsbad, California. I would always make sure I put a cap of $100 on my expenditure, and that included my greens fees and lunch. That way, on my worst days, I'd contain my losses to $25.

Still, the amount of the wager never mattered to Bobby. It was just the action. He enjoyed competing and always wanted to beat his opponent.

Bobby would also show up to my Bible study group. He'd always come with the same question: "Can a hustler like me ever make it to Heaven? Can God ever forgive me?" He always brought that up.

We focused on what sells in Phoenix, Arizona. We had Chris Evert, Kristien Kemmer Shaw, and Stephanie Tolleson as our female players. Our men were Tony Roche, Ross Case, and Butch Waltz. It just so happened that the girls were all very attractive. We became the fashion models of the tennis world. We had these three gorgeous blondes on our team. Chris even helped design the tennis dresses. It was all great for attendance.

We had a good thing going. Chrissie, Kristien, and Stephanie were best friends. Chrissie lived in a condo on Camelback Mountain. She would drive her friends around town in her Porsche. They worked on their tans.

Chrissie was the star of the show. Everyone wanted to talk to her. Everyone wanted to watch her play. We had to put boundaries on her media appearances and the promotional things we were doing. Chrissie helped us draw around 7,500 fans per match. It was well above the league average, even if a lot of those tickets were comps and giveaways. We had to produce a crowd, expose people to our product.

Chrissie and I had a great relationship. When I visited her and her father in Fort Lauderdale, I promised Jimmy Evert that I would look after his daughter. Like the time she had tendinitis and didn't want to play in an upcoming match against Cleveland.

I called their owner, Joe Zingale and said, "I'm sorry, but Chrissie can't play." And he went nuts. He had his law firm call me. He threatened to sue me. He said his fans bought tickets to see Chrissie play. But I stuck up for her. I think she appreciated that.

Here's what Chrissie once told *Newsweek* magazine about our relationship: "Jimmy was deeply religious and into his family. He would suggest we attend Bible study with him. I went once, and I left with a wonderful feeling of calm. That night, I lost to a girl that I never lost to. I never went again. I realized I needed to be a little bitchy to win."

During her first season with the Racquets, I asked Chrissie if she would team up with famed Olympian Jesse Owens, conducting a tennis clinic for 300 African-American boys and girls at the Salvation Army. I told her how Jesse won a gold medal at the 1936 Berlin Olympics while performing in front of Adolf Hitler. She had never done something like that before and she was fabulous. She was trying to teach proper groundstroke techniques and the kids kept hitting the tennis ball like it was a baseball. But Chris had tremendous patience, and the event was a smashing success.

As an owner, I tried to give my players their space. I always tried to encourage them. We had a few social gatherings at my house. I just tried to show my players a lot of respect.

After we blew a match in Oakland, I was really upset. I took a long walk around the arena to cool off. I went forty-five rows up in one of the end zones, and when I turned around, I saw another guy walking up the stairs. That guy was Cotton Fitzsimmons, former head coach of the Phoenix Suns.

He could see that I was extremely unhappy. I told him we really should've won that match and that I wanted to go down and talk to our players. He put his hand on my shoulder.

"Let me tell you something," Cotton said. "I know you're really upset. But, Jimmy, you don't need to talk to the players. You need to stay away from them right now. It's too emotional and it will not help you."

I took some advice from the expert.

Our 1976 team went 30-14, the second-best record in the WTT. Evert won Female MVP and Female Rookie of the Year awards. We lost to the Golden Gaters in the playoff semifinals.

We won the West division for a second consecutive year in 1977, playing at Veterans Memorial Stadium. We brought in palm trees and live music. On some nights, we outdrew the Phoenix Suns.

We drew a whopping 10,515 people for a match against Robert Kraft's franchise, the Boston Lobsters, which featured Evert's main rival, Martina Navratilova. We set a new record three weeks later, drawing 11,294 for the deciding match of the 1977 WTT championship series against the New York Apples. Reigning Wimbledon champ Virginia Wade got the better of Chrissie that day.

Along the way, I became the principal owner of the Racquets. Reggie was too busy with his playing career and Gary needed to focus on his sports agency and real estate businesses. It was daunting.

I found a strong ally in Dr. Jerry Buss, the former chemist turned real estate investor. We became close friends almost immediately. Jerry was very smart and definitely flamboyant. He had an incredible vision for the future and a sharp business mind. You could tell that I was his favorite.

If I needed to see him, I knew to show up in the hotel lobby at 4:00 a.m. That's when he was getting back from the clubs. He was always late to our official gatherings because he had been out partying the night before.

As soon as Jerry Buss bought into the NBA with the Lakers, I gave my dear friend and Suns owner Jerry Colangelo the following scouting report:

> Jerry, this is what's going to happen. Jerry Buss will come to the meeting late. He'll have a couple of young girls with him. He'll be quiet for the first half of the meeting, maybe even the first day. He won't say a word. But once things get going, he'll roll up his sleeves and go to work at the chalkboard, mapping out league strategy and things he feels are important.

In the WTT, not everyone listened to him because they were owners, and guys with big money have really big egos.

Jerry Buss also had better luck than I did. My team had the great Chris Evert. We led the WTT in attendance. Yet somehow, I lost about $2 million in my role as general partner.

We had some big contracts, but I didn't go into the venture as a classic rich boy to begin with. I was just a hard worker from the insurance business. At one point, Reggie said I was keeping the franchise together with Band-Aids.

At another point during my ownership, I was seriously undercapitalized. I needed a $50,000 line of credit just to be seated at a WTT league meeting. I couldn't pull it off. I was embarrassed and humbled. The guy who signed Evert to a two-year contract couldn't even be seated at the league meeting.

During that meeting, the owners were getting really rough with me. But Buss had my back. He stood up and said, "Hold on. Jimmy went out and put us on the map by signing the number one tennis player in the world." They argued a lot. That's what owners do when they get together. And that's when Buss said to the entire room, "I believe in Jimmy. And I'm going to back him."

He walked out of the meeting. Then he and I went for coffee and he told me he would cover me for the $50,000. You don't forget gestures like that. Especially when I had only known him for three weeks.

Meanwhile, Robert Kraft was a young man trying to make a name for himself in the WTT. He became an instant hit by shipping fresh lobster from Boston for all of our executive meetings.

Kraft said he learned a lot during the WTT. His franchise played at Walter Brown Arena, which is part of Boston University. He would pay for advertising and he would pay for his players. The school would get the parking revenue, the concessions, and all the sponsorship deals. All Kraft received was the ticket revenue.

He realized that was the wrong approach and the least profitable path. And when he purchased the Patriots, he did exactly the opposite. He built them from the other direction, taking control of the land, the stadium, and the parking lots first.

Both Buss and Kraft effectively served their internships in the WTT and look at what those two accomplished. Are there two bigger names in sports ownership?

Alas, in the early days of the WTT, we were doomed by the lack of television money. We had all the great female players, but we couldn't lure any of the top men. We tried for John McEnroe. We tried for Jimmy Connors. They were unavailable. Do you remember those great tennis matches they used to play at Caesar's Palace?

They were paying casino money to guys like McEnroe and Connors. We couldn't compete with that. We also had scheduling problems. We tried to fit a forty-four-match schedule into the soft spots on the professional tour. It wasn't easy, and we had to shut down operations for two weeks during Wimbledon.

Through the hard times, I continued to focus on building relationships with the players we had. Chris Evert once said about me:

> The special thing about Jimmy when I played for the Phoenix Racquets was that it wasn't about the wins. It wasn't about the tennis. With him, it was about the person. He's very religious. Other teams would play matches and go party or go to discos. With Jimmy, you played matches and then he'd invite you to a Bible study. I always felt with Jimmy it was about getting to that next layer with the team, about going deeper and getting to know the person, who they are, how they are doing, where they are in their life. It wasn't a superficial relationship where, "OK, I signed you for $100,000, and I expect you to get me tennis results." He was a different kind of owner from day one.

In 1976, I tried to create a marketing bonanza for the WTT. One of the teams in our league was the Soviet Union. Our league was also young and needed instant credibility. I felt the Phoenix Racquets could gain some momentum and important publicity by playing the Soviet Union in Plains, Georgia, the hometown of sitting President Jimmy Carter.

Carter's brother, Billy, was almost as famous for much different reasons. I reached Billy on the telephone at his gas station in Plains. I told him my plans, how we had the number one women's tennis player in the world. I told him we would draw a big audience and donate some of the profits to build two tennis courts in Plains, a city that didn't have any tennis courts. I told him we would build these courts in the park adjacent to President Carter's home.

A few days later, I was in Georgia, finalizing plans with Billy Carter. Plains was truly in the middle of nowhere. I pulled up to a gas station and was astounded to see the president's brother pumping gas. We had dinner at the Elks Club in Americus, the town that borders Plains. I will not share how many beers Billy drank that night, but I can safely say it was a lot.

We accomplished our mission. We built two new tennis courts in Plains, Georgia. The night before our match with the Soviet Union, we staged a dinner at Miss Lillian's Pond House, a restaurant named after Carter's mother and where the president officially chose his cabinet. We arranged a celebrity tennis match that included Billy Carter, Bobby Riggs, and Chris Evert.

We drew 4,000 people to our event on the brand-new tennis courts in Plains, Georgia. We also drew enormous media coverage, which was very important. The event inspired a few words from President Carter, who said, "I enjoyed the tennis courts made available for this event. It was highly publicized, and Billy really enjoyed it."

In the end, there was too much politics in tennis. There were other startup leagues, like World Championship Tennis. There were always scheduling problems, issues with agents, issues with everything.

Evert's two-year deal expired after the 1977 season. She went on to sign with our rival, the Los Angeles Strings. Early in 1978, I was tapped out. We sold the Racquets to a local petroleum dealer, Jerry Simmons, who was one of my best friends.

My attorney and many others advised me to declare bankruptcy. I wouldn't do that. I couldn't do that. I set a goal to pay back every cent to every creditor. Bankruptcy would have been the easy way to deal with my debt, but it didn't interest me and never entered my mind.

Some of my creditors received $1,000 per month. Some received $100 a month. All of them received something in the mail, every month, from Jimmy Walker. Some were receiving checks for fifteen years, but everyone was paid back in full. I am proud of that. It was not easy.

Over the years, I kept in touch with Jerry Buss. After he purchased the Lakers, he chose me to be his insurance broker. I wrote jumbo policies on star players like Kareem Abdul-Jabbar, Magic Johnson, Norm Nixon, Michael Cooper, and James Worthy. I was his guest anytime I wanted to see a Lakers game in person or hang in the celebrity-infested Forum Club. I was his guest so often that tickets were no longer necessary. Everyone knew I was a close friend of Dr. Buss. I came and went as I chose.

Like Reggie had, Buss opened a lot of doors for me.

Buss introduced me to Clippers owner Donald Sterling, who introduced me to famed comedian Billy Crystal, who wrote the foreword to this book, and whom I introduced to the greatest heavyweight boxer in history, Muhammad Ali. Both Sterling and Crystal remain life insurance clients to this day. More on them later.

In the WTT, I never stopped swinging for the fences.

I kept trying new angles. Remember John Lucas, the former basketball star? He was also known as a great tennis player and a great leader. He was the number one overall pick by the Houston Rockets in the 1976 NBA draft. He had broken Pete Maravich's high school scoring record in North Carolina and was also a U.S. Junior Davis Cup member. He had received 401 college scholarship offers— reportedly 350 in basketball and fifty-one in tennis.

I decided to sign Lucas. We verbally agreed on $25,000 compensation for three months of tennis. The deal was done within twenty-four hours.

But then I changed my mind.

I knew we needed someone bigger to move the meter, a box office presence to capture the imagination. I heard that Dean Martin Jr. was a great tennis player. He was also the son of an American icon. He was very popular and very handsome. If I could market him while enticing his father and Frank Sinatra to come to a match in Phoenix, I'd be sitting on a goldmine.

Lucas was very upset with my change of heart. He was represented by a young agent by the name of David Falk, who was also extremely unhappy.

"You can't do that," Falk said. "John is livid. His family is upset. You had a deal!"

That was true. We had a deal. But there was nothing in writing. I could have easily washed my hands and walked away unscathed. I chose to honor my word. We ended up settling on $18,000, even though Lucas never hit a tennis ball for the Racquets. And in those days, $18,000 was a significant chunk of money. It turned out to be a game-changing decision for me, even though I had no idea at the time.

Dean Martin Jr. eventually played for the Racquets, but I could never get his famous father to attend our matches or have a few cocktails. Dean Martin lived in Las Vegas but he wouldn't hop on a plane, even though Dean Jr. wanted him to come badly. It was kind of sad. It was even sadder when Dean Jr. died in a plane crash in 1987 at the age of thirty-five.

They said Dean Martin was never the same again.

Unfortunately, I would come to know that same awful feeling many years later.

CHAPTER 4

PUTTING ON THE RITZ

Courting Pro Athletes and Entertainers

*M*ICHAEL JORDAN IS A SUPERSTAR. HE HAD MANY PEOPLE looking out for his interests during his spectacular NBA career.

I made sure he always had a black Mercedes-Benz waiting for him when he checked into the Phoenix Ritz-Carlton hotel whenever his Bulls were in town playing the Phoenix Suns.

The luxury car was his gift from me. It was a temporary gift, of course. But it was always there. Always waiting in the valet parking lot at the Ritz.

It helped me grow a relationship with the most popular athlete on the planet.

The car was there for him as a rookie in 1984. It was there for him during the NBA Finals in 1993 when Jordan's Bulls beat Charles

Barkley's Suns in a thrilling six-game series. It was there for him whenever he showed up in Arizona—for as long as he remained in town.

I understood the mentality of professional athletes. I understood their need to feel special. I spent my life dreaming of their reality. I knew what they wanted because at one time, I wanted it even more.

These young men are incredibly wealthy and pampered. Decadence becomes their new normal. They fly on private jets. They avoid security screenings at commercial airports. They aren't forced to take off their shoes or put laptops in a separate bin.

It gets even better when they land. Buses are waiting for them on the tarmac. Someone else is carrying their luggage. People wait in lobbies to hand out room keys as they walk into hotels. Professional athletes can check in to their five-star rooms without breaking stride. They are also paid per diems, daily pocket money they can use on meals or public transportation.

So what are they missing on the road?

They are missing freedom, control, and anonymity. They are missing the options that come with having their own vehicle in a random city, with no paperwork or strings attached. They are missing the ability to disappear without a trace, without anyone knowing their business. Even if it is just a few priceless moments.

I knew all the valets at the Ritz. I tipped them very well. They made sure the keys to that luxury car were always there waiting for my highest-profile clients.

Even if the car never left the parking lot, the gesture was all that mattered. It was an incredibly effective marketing tool. It always left a lasting impression.

I first left a vehicle for Dr. J and Charles Barkley when they played for the Philadelphia 76ers. Here's what Barkley once said about our arrangement:

"Jimmy and I met under strange circumstances," Barkley said. "I thought he was a weird guy when I first met him. I was playing for the 76ers, and every time we played in Phoenix, there was a Mercedes-Benz at the hotel for Dr. J to drive around. After Doc retired, when I checked into the hotel, there was a Mercedes-Benz waiting for me. I thought, *Are you kidding me?* I never took it because I didn't know the situation."

"Doc caught up to me and said, 'Hey, you never drive that car while you're in Phoenix?'"

"I said, 'Doc, I got no idea what you're talking about.'"

"He said, 'My good friend, Jimmy Walker, always left me a Mercedes and now he's leaving it for you.'"

I left that car for a lot of players including Shawn Bradley, who stood seven foot six and was one of the tallest players in NBA history. I picked up the vehicle after Shawn left town and the driver's seat leaned all the way back. I mean, all the way. You have no other options when you are seven foot six!

The same was true with Shaq. Whenever the Lakers came to Phoenix to play the Suns, he would practically move the driver's seat in the trunk so he could fit in the car.

Obviously, Jordan was a huge potential client. He was also meticulous about his corporate image and how he presented himself in public. His business partners wore their association with Jordan like badges of honor. Nobody spoke out of school. He was a force in competitive sports and commerce, on and off the court.

Jordan was also very guarded. He had to be careful, considering his meteoric rise and how many people wanted a piece of him. He was also very loyal.

After he was drafted by the Bulls in 1984, Jordan arrived at O'Hare airport in Chicago as the new kid in the big city. He couldn't find his prearranged ride. Instead, he came upon a limousine driver named George Kohler, who was hopelessly waiting on a fare that never showed up. They met by fate. They needed each other.

Legend has it that George quickly put his foot in his mouth. He asked Michael if his name was Larry Jordan.

Turns out, Larry was also the name of Jordan's older brother, and Kohler's innocent mistake had a dramatic effect.

George offered a $25 flat rate to chauffer Michael to his hotel. Jordan agreed and left with Kohler's business card. They became close friends overnight. The story of their relationship proves something I've experienced and learned over the years: the eternal, unmistakable, unpredictable, irreplaceable value of human connection. Of reaching out and taking chances. Of not feeling inhibited or paralyzed by the fear of rejection. All the great stuff that comes with expanding your horizons and meeting new people.

Identifying the needs of celebrity clients requires even deeper understanding. You must know and recognize the bubbles and fishbowls in which they live and work. Most celebrities have access to everything life has to offer. But they enjoy very little of our most basic freedoms. We see them as lottery winners. They feel like victims and martyrs.

They are exalted to the point of exhaustion. They feel blessed by it all, but they also crave an anonymity that will never, ever return to them while they're in the spotlight. Their needs are not normal because their lives are not normal. Their fans won't allow that to happen. We need them to be bigger than life. They want to be bigger than life. That is what makes them celebrities.

To cope, celebrities learn to put up walls. They find it hard to trust. They can be some of the most empty, insecure people you'll ever meet. They are also looking for signs that go beyond the superficial, signs that represent real connections and real relationships. They grow weary of people who are constantly asking for favors and financial assistance. They learn to trust the handful of people in their lives who ask for nothing.

I made it a point to ask for nothing.

Over and over again, I asked for nothing.

Asking for nothing is a great policy with every new relationship. And there is no quicker path to credibility with celebrities.

Because I asked for nothing in return, Jordan would always leave something in that Mercedes as a thank-you note: an autographed basketball, a pair of shoes, a jersey, maybe a practice T-shirt. Something to show his appreciation.

I also had one other bargaining chip when it came to Jordan, one that I had earned during my short tenure as World Team Tennis owner.

As I described in the previous chapter, I had backtracked on my verbal commitment to sign NBA star John Lucas to a part-time tennis contract. I infuriated his young agent, David Falk, who let me know in very plain terms how disappointed they were in my actions. Their anger quickly subsided when I chose to pay Lucas nearly 75 percent of his contract.

It was a benevolent gesture on my part. I did so out of fairness, to honor the spirit of our agreement. I did so because that is the kind of owner and person I wanted to be—and because that's the way I was raised.

My dad would always say, "You don't get credit for being honest. It's what is expected of you." He was a big fan of the handshake deal. He stressed to me how important it is to be truthful and stick to your word. He was right. That's what I did with John Lucas, and in the process, I strengthened relationships that would help serve as the foundation of my business.

Shortly after I paid Lucas his $18,000, I received a call from Falk.

He said, "Jimmy, I owe you a favor. No NBA owner I've worked with would have ever done something like that, how you honored a verbal commitment to John Lucas. I respect how you kept your word when we had nothing in writing."

Falk soon became Michael Jordan's agent and primary business advisor. To this day, Michael Jordan owns one of the biggest life insurance policies I have ever written for a professional athlete. He has always been one of my best clients. He has been loyal to keep his insurance program with me in force to this date. Michael also has an excellent business advisor in Curtis Polk.

During the early stages of his career with Bulls, I remember picking up Jordan at the airport. He needed a physical exam for his life insurance policy. I promised him there would be no publicity, no adoring fans, and no autograph seekers.

I personally contacted the cardiologist. I told him the rules. He assured me he understood. And when Jordan and I showed up, the doctor's son and fifteen of his classmates were waiting in the reception area.

But our relationship remained strong. It is amazing how things work out when you make decisions for the right reasons, based on strong convictions and principles, like I did with one of Falk's early clients, before he signed up with the greatest basketball player in history.

Nevertheless, I felt a great deal of pressure after Jordan retired from the NBA in 1993, when he was attempting to carve out a new career in Major League Baseball. He was coming back to the Valley to play for the Scottsdale Scorpions in the Arizona Fall League, an annual proving ground for young baseball prospects. I was the guy who'd always provided him with a vehicle in the past. And given his prolonged upcoming stay, I knew I had to come up with something special.

"What do you want to drive, Michael?" I asked.

"A Range Rover," he said without blinking.

Immediately, I went on a quest to provide Jordan with his own Range Rover. I cut a deal with a local Lexus dealership. I strongly encouraged the owner not to bother Jordan for favors or seek any additional media attention. I told them it was important to give without asking for anything in return, to let the publicity and good-will come to them over the course of time. The strategy always requires restraint and patience, but I have learned that it almost always works.

Sure enough, a *Sports Illustrated* story appeared on Michael Jordan and the Arizona Fall League that highlighted the Range Rover gifted to him from a Scottsdale Lexus dealership. You could not buy that kind of advertising.

Jordan was the biggest star on the planet. And growing a clientele base of over one hundred professional athletes helped me better understand the dynamics of celebrity life in America.

Originally, my office was located on the eighth floor of a Phoenix high-rise. The views were great. Until I realized the fatal flaw: too many celebrity clients don't have the patience or the desire to travel vertically. They don't want to be trapped inside elevators, along with the awkward moments that ensue, just to visit the eighth floor of a high-rise office. It immediately puts them on the defensive and in a bad mood.

I soon realized I didn't need a sweeping view. I didn't need to see mountains or sunsets on the horizon. I needed views from the ground floor, allowing me to see what I'd been missing underneath my nose, to recruit the unexpected celebrities suddenly standing in line for coffee. Or the lobby full of millionaire athletes who just arrived for an NBA game in Phoenix. I needed them to have easy in-and-out access.

In 1998, we leased space on the ground floor of that very same building. Our patio was fifty feet from a bustling Starbucks. We were 200 feet from the lobby of the Ritz-Carlton, located in the swank Biltmore shopping district. It was a tremendous location. Our real estate clients told us repeatedly that we had the best single office location in Phoenix. And I made the most of it.

You want hustle? Whenever visiting NBA teams flew into Phoenix, I would be there, outside and waiting, whenever the team bus came to a stop. I would seek out certain players. I would make small talk. I would reintroduce myself to those who might remember me from the previous season.

Some were friendly in return. Some would blow me off. It didn't matter to me. You were in the game or you weren't. Besides, as Billy Crystal once said, I knew how to take a punch.

It took a lot of boldness to operate the way I did. It certainly took a lot of effort. But over time, I built up a client base of over one hundred professional athletes. Most of them drove my Mercedes at one point or another.

Maybe recruiting celebrity performers was easier back in the day, before athletes could remove themselves from reality and human interaction simply by wearing headphones or earbuds. But I think I would do just as well in today's world. Maybe even better. And it wasn't that easy back in the good old days.

After Kevin Garnett became a client of mine, we met at Houston's restaurant in Scottsdale. I'll never forget because Garnett ordered three hot fudge sundaes that afternoon—and he arrived wearing headphones, which made it hard to communicate with him about his retirement plans and his future.

Business was so brisk at the time that I had to buy a secondary luxury car. Sometimes, I'd end up leaving the backup vehicle at the Ritz-Carlton as well. That required taking a cab home from work because all my personal cars were all taken. You learn to do what the game requires.

I also left the car for St. Louis Cardinals star Mark McGwire. The slugger would always leave me an autographed bat or glove. When I learned that Warren Buffett was a huge Cardinals fan, I sent him the autographed McGwire glove. He liked that a lot.

By the way, in all my years supplying NBA stars with a comped Mercedes, I only had one player who actually paid me for gas. His name was Jerome Kersey, a muscular power forward who played seventeen seasons in the NBA.

Jerome always left me cash inside the vehicle when he drove my car. He left me $25 with a note: "Mr. Walker, here's some gas money. Thanks for the ride!"

I didn't expect that.

Former NBA star Damon Stoudemire once left me a note that read, "Jimmy, we locked the keys in the car. We had to get a locksmith. Sorry!"

I would have never known the difference. But Stoudemire was probably raised like I was, where telling the truth was important and expected at all times.

Besides, when you are leaving a luxury car for young, rich, and famous alpha male professional athletes, you also budget for testosterone and mishaps. I expected the occasional nicks, scratches, and dings to my Mercedes-Benz.

The biggest problem I encountered was with an extremely famous client who will remain unnamed. The one who left used condoms in my car.

Try explaining that to your wife.

CHAPTER 5

SWIMMING WITH SHARKS

Meeting Big Names in Big Business

P ROFESSIONAL ATHLETES ARE GREAT, BUT THEIR LEVEL OF fame can be unwieldy. Dealing with their agents can be sticky business. It's cut-throat, bottom-line industry. There's not a ton of loyalty. Athletes frequently change their agents, and sometimes the new representative comes in and completely changes the dynamics of an existing relationship. Sometimes they'll even take your policy, steering athletes to other insurance brokers. And then the new agents will take a commission or a finder's fee for changing their client's insurance program. I have seen this happen too many times.

So I knew I needed to expand my horizons.

I badly wanted to meet Walmart founder Sam Walton. He was the modern-day J.C. Penney. He was the Elvis Presley and Michael

Jordan of retailing. He changed the way Americans spend their money.

I did what I do best.

I wrote him a letter congratulating him on his enormous success.

Within a week, I received a response from Walton. I quickly discovered Sam was prolific at writing letters, just like me. His letters were warm and friendly. After exchanging eight to nine pieces of correspondence, I grew bold and called for a meeting.

Pro tip: Most every CEO or celebrity has a gatekeeper, an executive assistant who is in charge of schedules and appointments. A gatekeeper filters calls, letters, emails, and office visitors. It's critically important to get on the good side of gatekeepers because they can make or break you. And they know it.

I did my homework. I became friendly with Sam's gatekeeper, an executive assistant named Becky Elliott. I called her several times just to get acquainted, building a foundation of trust. She already knew who I was because she had been typing the letters Sam would send to me. I told her I was traveling back east and broached the idea of swinging by Bentonville, Arkansas, for a visit with Sam.

"Jimmy," she said. "Why don't I put this call through to Sam and you can speak with him directly?"

I took a deep breath.

Sam was an American icon. He was born on an Oklahoma farm and grew up through the Great Depression. He bought his first variety store in Bentonville, where he brought all of his ideas to life, the ones that got him kicked out of job meetings with Ben Franklin franchising executives.

Using ingenuity and creativity, Sam reconfigured the supply chain. He bought in bulk, offered lower prices to consumers, and provided easy access to goods. He recognized the underserved customers in rural areas all across America. His stores kept getting bigger and bigger, and so did his personal fortune. But he kept a close connection with his customers. He even learned to fly his own plane so he could visit multiple stores in the same day.

"There is only one boss. The customer. And he can fire everybody in the company from the chairman on down, simply by spending his money somewhere else," Walton famously said.

I felt like we had a lot in common. His fundamental beliefs on leadership essentially mirrored my own.

"Outstanding leaders go out of their way to boost the self-esteem of their personnel," Walton once said. "If people believe in themselves, it's amazing what they can accomplish."

My first conversation with Sam could not have gone any better. We agreed to meet for breakfast in Bentonville. He recommended I stay at the Days Inn.

"It's not much," Walton said. "But it is all Bentonville has to offer."

Five minutes later, Becky called me back. She informed me of a much nicer hotel in a neighboring city, a Holiday Inn located halfway between Bentonville and Fayetteville. The offer was tempting, but I had a moment of clarity. No way was I going to upstage Sam Walton and stay at the Holiday Inn. If Sam Walton recommends the Days Inn, well, that's where I'm staying.

We met at my hotel. Sam arrived at 7:00 a.m. He drove a pickup truck and his dog was in the back. You could see instantly how grounded he was, and how he never lost touch or sight of his customers.

We met in the lobby and walked around the coffee shop. Everybody recognized him. He shook hands with everyone in the restaurant. He autographed $1 bills. At one point, Sam asked if he could get in trouble with the United States government for defacing so much money with his signature.

"Sam, I wouldn't worry," I said. "I think you are safe."

With Sam, the customer was always number one. The customer was always right. When you walk into a Walmart, there is always someone greeting you at the front door with a smile. If you need a book, a paper clip, a gallon of milk, or a garden hose, they will happily escort you to the proper section of the store. You can never underestimate the importance of treating your customer as the most important person in your business life.

From 1982–88, Sam was ranked as the richest person in America. He had a net worth of $8.6 billion when died in 1992. But he never thought he was better than anyone else. Instead, he was all about customers and relationships. When you met Sam Walton, you knew immediately that he was the king of hospitality.

During our meeting, Sam told me about his four-year-old grandson, Luke, who was ill. He was also a huge Michael Jordan fan.

When I left our meeting, I contacted Jordan. I told him about Walton's grandson. I asked if he wouldn't mind sending along an autographed basketball for young Luke. Michael obliged, and I gave that ball to Sam. I love being a facilitator in situations like that, connecting a pair of megawatt celebrities with a simple gesture.

I also learned the value of humility from Sam. He was one of the most successful business leaders in the world and yet he carried himself without a hint of arrogance or elitism. He was not full of himself and driven by ego like so many other successful entrepreneurs.

That is why he referred to his employees as "associates." He wanted the person in charge of cleaning the bathroom or sweeping the parking lot to feel just as important as a senior executive at Walmart. He wanted everyone to feel like a partner. Sam Walton believed in the power of teamwork and he was a great leader.

Sam often held a Saturday morning meeting at his Bentonville store, where his empire first started. It was the equivalent of a weekly pep rally. Attendance was not required, but many of his associates came to hear him speak at the Walmart Auditorium. He said it was his favorite meeting of the week. He really enjoyed giving motivational talks and inspirational speeches.

Sam reinforced my beliefs about leadership, the importance of encouragement, and showing appreciation for people who work behind the scenes. Your associates will work harder for you and derive greater enjoyment from their work when you fill them with positive feedback rather than bombarding them with constant nagging and criticism.

We all make mistakes. Sam understood that and found the best in every person. He instilled that in me.

❁ ❀ ❁ ❀ ❁

Billy Joe "Red" McCombs was another one of my high-profile business contacts. He founded the Red McCombs Automotive Group, building a network of over fifty car dealerships in Texas. He cofounded radio giant Clear Channel Communications, which he used as an advertising platform for his automobile empire. He was once the majority owner of the San Antonio Spurs, the Denver Nuggets, and the Minnesota Vikings.

I met Red nearly four decades ago and kept in touch over the years. He always answered my calls. I always wanted him as a client, but we rarely talked about business. In fact, I knew him for twenty-five years before he became my client. But I never gave up—probably because I didn't know better. For some reason, I always thought opportunity was just around the corner with Red, even if it took a quarter-century.

After we finished our deal, Red praised me for my persistence and patience. Just like a sports owner, he applauded me for "staying in the batter's box." McCombs said of our relationship:

Jimmy has a very engaging personality. He's the kind of guy who always makes you feel better after you have visited with him on anything. From the first time Jimmy contacted me about an insurance product, which I didn't have any interest in, he regularly contacted me over a twenty-year period.

Finally, we did one of the biggest programs he's ever written. The reason I contacted Jimmy when we finally got together to do something was because I wanted someone who was intensely interested in me and someone who was professionally always on top of the game. Jimmy, two to three times a year, would contact me to compliment or praise something I was interested in.

We never talked business. He has a very low-key and pleasant way of staying in touch with people. When you get a call from him, you want to accept it because it's always a very positive call. It's more than patience. It says to me he really cares. That impresses you. I didn't hesitate to call him when I was ready. I didn't call two or three brokers to get bids. I knew he'd have the best proposal in the industry. I was comfortable with it and felt like he was working for me.

Yes, my patience paid off with Red. But the key is keeping in touch, which is one of the tenets of my life—one of the foundational pillars of my business success.

My approach doesn't always work. Sometimes, I'm guilty of overdoing it and keeping in touch too often.

Thomas Edison once said: "I haven't failed. I've identified 10,000 ways why this doesn't work." I have found this to be true in my own relationships with high-profile clients, and I've learned from some of my mistakes.

My own light bulb went on after I scored a meeting with media titan Rupert Murdoch at his office in New York. And I blew it.

I had written Murdoch several letters. I referenced my affinity for a book—Rick Warren's *The Purpose Driven Life*, which had been published by one of the many companies owned by Murdoch.

I reached out to Murdoch's gatekeeper and asked for a meeting to discuss Warren's book. I never mentioned I was going to discuss any business matters.

It was natural for me to talk about the book. I loved the message, and the book was equally fascinating to Murdoch, mostly because it reached enormous levels of success, selling more than 30 million copies at the time.

I asked for fifteen minutes of his time to discuss the book. He agreed.

Murdoch's phone rang several times during our meeting. Each time he answered, but immediately said he would return their call. He did not allow for interruptions in our meeting, which was impressive.

When I stood up after my allotted fifteen minutes had expired, he asked me to sit back down and stay a while. He was clearly enjoying our visit regarding *The Purpose Driven Life*.

I took an icy plunge. I shifted the subject to my business, telling him how we specialized in families with high net worth, and how we already helped numerous wealthy families with their estate planning needs.

Rupert was polite, but the air was coming out of the balloon. I could see he was fast losing interest in our conversation. I should have stayed on subject, but I didn't. I crossed a line and became too aggressive with my agenda, which clearly did not include any business discussions.

I thanked him for his time, and once I returned to Phoenix, I followed up by sending a thank you note. I've tried to meet with Rupert again on various occasions during my many trips to New York but have not succeeded in receiving a second meeting.

I believe my clumsiness in mixing business with a book discussion created a situation where he lost respect for me. I can understand why he might have been confused or felt misled about the purpose of our meeting.

Regardless, I was out of bounds. I goofed. My timing and judgment were poor, and I learned the importance of making a better first impression by sticking to the agenda.

Like most people, I've learned more from my mistakes and failures than I've learned from success. Mistakes are going to happen. I believe there is no disgrace in failing or losing in life, not when you've done your best while trying to do the right thing.

It's important to look in the mirror when mistakes occur. To self-scout and analyze what went wrong. Like any coach or player, I spend time reviewing my turnovers. The best coaches know if you limit turnovers and commit fewer than your opponent, you'll likely win the game.

Tiger Woods is arguably the greatest golfer of all time. And he's changed his swing three times! Then there's Michael Jordan, who succinctly said, "I've failed over and over again playing basketball. And that is why I succeed."

That tells you change is not a luxury. It's a necessity.

Or as the late, great Ben Feldman once said while becoming a prolific life insurance salesman, "A fool learns from experience. A wise man learns from the experiences of others."

I have also had a long journey with Donald Sterling. He was a client referred to me by Dr. Jerry Buss, who owned the Lakers. Sterling built his fortune in real estate and was the former owner of the Los Angeles Clippers.

I made a mistake during one of our visits in Sterling's office. As I was reviewing Sterling's insurance program, Don abruptly changed the subject. He was trying to re-sign starting forward Ken Norman, who was represented by the NBA's premier agent and my close friend, David Falk. Don thought Falk's financial demands were outrageous, and discussions between the two had become very heated.

During our meeting, I made the mistake of giving my opinion of Norman as a basketball player, telling Don that the Clippers needed to re-sign Norman immediately. I said I trusted Sterling was doing everything he could make a new contract happen, and Falk was surely doing the same on the other side of the bargaining table.

Don looked at me with a puzzled look. He expressed his frustrations with Falk, who was known for getting top dollar for his marquee clients. These were two highly successful men. Falk rose to stardom by representing Michael Jordan. Don was proving to be a real estate genius with all his Beverly Hills acquisitions. And suddenly, their relationship was seriously frayed.

I thought I could help, but I was very wrong.

"Don, if you look at it from David's standpoint, he's merely trying to do his job by getting his client fair market value," I said.

Don glared at me. He said he didn't think David was being fair at all. I told him there were two sides to every story, but he didn't like the way David was handling the negotiations, and he certainly did not appreciate me sticking up for Falk. He also knew Falk was a friend of mine, and that some of Falk's clients had insurance policies with me.

The more I talked, the more infuriated Sterling became.

"Jimmy, there is the door. Get out of my office!" he roared.

I stood up.

"Don, I'm sorry you feel this way but ..." I responded.

"Get out!" he screamed.

Just like that, the owner of the Clippers had kicked me out of his beautiful, spacious office on Rodeo Drive. I was embarrassed and humiliated.

I remained outwardly calm, even though I had never been thrown out of an office before. I knew I blew it by opening my big mouth. I should've listened to Don's frustrations with an agent without interfering, especially when Don had reasons to question my motives.

I cut my losses and left with my head down. Don never brought it up again.

It was not my finest moment.

But after all these years of hustling and grinding, here is what I've learned about mistakes:

- We all fail. Don't throw away your mistakes. You can learn from them.
- Don't let your mistakes make you bitter. Let your mistakes make you better.
- There are two kinds of mistakes: people who will do nothing they are told and the people who will do nothing else.
- Some mistakes are more triumphant than victories.
- You must have long-range goals to keep you from being frustrated by short-term mistakes.
- Someone who commits a mistake and doesn't correct that mistake is making yet another mistake.
- Staying calm is the key to overcoming mistakes.

Most of the successful people I've met in business, sports, and entertainment have all consistently failed before reaching their true potential.

It's okay to make some mistakes because it's proof you're actually trying. My dad taught me that one.

Finally, if you learn from your mistakes, they might not be mistakes at all.

And if you're really lucky, your biggest mistakes will happen on a golf course. Mine are called mulligans.

CHAPTER 6

UNLEASHING CHARLES BARKLEY

Fight Night Takes Flight

JERRY COLANGELO IS THE GODFATHER OF ARIZONA SPORTS. He is a great man with great vision and a great heart. He came to the Valley with three kids, nine suitcases, and $300 in his pocket—hired to help launch an NBA team in Phoenix. He ended up building an empire in the desert.

Colangelo and I are lifetime friends. When I met Jerry, he was just twenty-eight years old, the youngest general manager in the NBA. I wrote his insurance policies. I told him how excited the city of Phoenix was to have someone of his pedigree, an executive who helped launch the Chicago Bulls.

After just three weeks in Phoenix, Jerry told me the Suns needed a booster club. He said I was going to be the president. Having been around twenty-one at the time, I felt I had died and gone to Heaven—that is how important it was to me.

For eternity, I will remain the first president of the Phoenix Suns Boosters Club.

Colangelo and I work extremely well together. In all our years as friends, he never says no to me. I reciprocate by never saying no to him.

I bought two season tickets to watch the Suns. I sat on the floor in the first row. For twenty-five years, I gained a reputation for creating a buzz inside the arena by bringing an assortment of celebrity friends to watch games with me.

People in attendance actually wondered, *Who will Jimmy Walker show up with tonight?*

I knew that Phoenix was a big-event, celebrity-obsessed town, so this was a great marketing tool for my business. It was a way to sustain relationships, as I had numerous NBA players who owned life insurance with me and played for other teams. Since I was seated on the floor, this gave me an opportunity to briefly visit with those clients during pre-game warmups.

Once, I took Olympic track and field star Carl Lewis to a Suns game. He was wearing pink leather shoes with four-inch heels. Kevin Johnson was a point guard or the Suns, and he noticed Lewis's shoes as he was dribbling the ball up court. Just before he drove the lane for a layup, he said, "Hey, Carl, love the shoes!"

It was great fun, and it all reached an apex during the 1992–93 NBA season.

Colangelo had already put Phoenix on the map. The NBA All-Star Game came to the Valley in 1975, putting compelling images of Arizona on national television: the saguaro cacti, the breathtaking sunsets, the Grand Canyon. One year later, the Suns made an improbable run to the 1976 NBA Finals against the Boston Celtics, capturing the imagination of basketball fans across the country.

In June 1992, Colangelo pulled off a blockbuster trade that reverberated through the NBA, acquiring Charles Barkley in multiplayer swap. The single transaction changed everything in Arizona.

Barkley was born in Alabama, he became an NBA star in Philadelphia, and in the early 1990s, he absolutely owned the city of Phoenix. He led the Suns to the 1993 NBA Finals, losing a six-game series to Michael Jordan's Bulls. But the end results weren't the only things that mattered. It was all about the show.

Barkley galvanized a growing region full of new Phoenix transplants. He made people laugh and said outlandish things. He was as fearless as he was funny. He was also frequently the lead story on nightly newscasts in Arizona, making Phoenix feel like it had finally reached the big time.

Around that time, I had a really big idea.

I called John Rolfs, who was the general manager of the Phoenix Ritz-Carlton.

"Why don't we do a charity event at the ballroom of the Ritz?" I asked. "We'll bring together a collection of celebrities led by Charles Barkley. They'll put on oversized boxing gloves. It'll be pure comedy, and we'll raise a lot of money. Charles owns Phoenix. Trust me, this won't miss."

Once I mentioned Barkley, it was a done deal.

I knew Charles had a heart of gold and was extremely charitable. This is a guy who would later announce that he was going to sell his MVP Trophy and Olympic memorabilia to build affordable housing in his hometown of Leeds, Alabama. He donated $200,000 to a South Lake Tahoe community that was ravaged by a wildfire. And he offered to pay for the funerals of three Philadelphians killed in a carjacking.

He has always had a soft spot in his heart for those less fortunate. He will give you the shirt off his back.

So I called Charles, explaining the nature of my charity event.

Knowing he was a huge boxing fan, I told him we wanted him to get inside the ring and fight Michael Carbajal, a five-time world boxing champion, a light flyweight legend who hailed from Phoenix.

"What?" he said. "You want me to fight Michael Carbajal?!"

Clearly, I had his attention.

"Charles," I said. "We are going to put you guys in oversized gloves. The gloves are so big that you can't get hurt. Other celebrities will be there. We'll have a life-size, real-deal boxing ring shipped in from Las Vegas and a signature bell. We'll make it look and sound like a real fight. We'll even use celebrity referees. And then we will give 60 percent of the proceeds to Michael Carbajal's boxing gym in Phoenix. What do you think?"

"I love it," he said. "When do you want me?"

Emboldened, I called Dan Majerle, the second-most popular player for the Suns. I began to explain the details of my event. A few words into my sales pitch, he interrupted me.

"I've already heard about it," Majerle said. "I'm in."

Just like that, we had the two most popular athletes in Phoenix as well as Michael Carbajal. We decided to call the event Fight Night. We purchased huge boxing gloves that looked like giant marshmallows, and we printed 400 tickets and sold out almost immediately.

"I was happy to get in the ring with large gloves and box with Charles Barkley," said Carbajal, a five-time world champion. "It was a lot of fun, and the good news is that the proceeds helped my 9th Street Gym, which benefitted many people in need."

We also hired Don Knotts to be our referee, an actor and comedian best known for his role as Deputy Sheriff Barney Fife on *The Andy Griffith Show*.

Our announcer was famed Suns broadcaster Al McCoy, who is in the Naismith Memorial Basketball Hall of Fame and the team's Ring of Honor. Al is also my cousin! True story. My aunt was Al McCoy's mother. At only six years old, I would sit on Al's

I was giving Reggie Jackson some hitting tips when Mr. October
played for the Oakland A's during spring training in 1973.

Magic Johnson and Isaiah Thomas told me Pistol Pete
Maravich created showtime in the NBA. I was a pallbearer at
Pete's funeral when he passed at the young age of forty.

Me, Jonnie, Gary, Meredith Ann, Dad, and
Mom. We were a very close family.

When I signed Chris Evert in 1976, she was the number one
women's tennis player in the world. When Chris signed to play
for our Phoenix Racquets, our attendance skyrocketed.

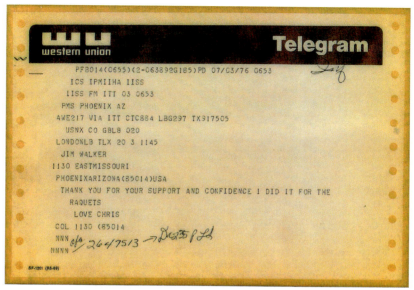

PFB014(0655)(2-063892G185)PD 07/03/76 0653
ICS IPMIIHA IISS
IISS FM ITT 03 0653
PMS PHOENIX AZ
AWE217 VIA ITT CTC884 LBG297 TX917505
USNX CO GBLB 020
LONDONLB TLX 20 3 1145
JIM WALKER
1130 EASTMISSOURI
PHOENIXARIZONA(85014)USA
THANK YOU FOR YOUR SUPPORT AND CONFIDENCE I DID IT FOR THE
RAQUETS
LOVE CHRIS
COL 1130 (85014
NNN
NNNN

Chris Evert was such a class act when she played for our Phoenix Racquets. She sent me a telegram minutes after she won Wimbledon in 1976 saying, "I did it for The Racquets."

Kenny Rogers was one of the nicest guys I have ever met. We played tennis and golf together throughout the years.

Always fun having Michael Jordan and his agent,
David Falk, join me at a Phoenix Suns game.

Amar'e Stoudemire saying hi to Muhammad and me at a Suns game.

Two winners—Muhammad Ali and his lovely wife, Lonnie

Tom Brady, with his friend Ryan Klesko, landed
a good punch on "The Champ."

Charles Barkley, five-time World Boxing Champion Michael Carbajal, and Dan Majerle boxing in the ballroom at the Phoenix Ritz-Carlton at our Celebrity Fight Night charity event.

Mini-Me knocked out Joe Montana. Jake Plummer is the coach with Dan Patrick announcing the boxing match.

Phil Mickelson and Billy Mayfair putting while referees Alice Cooper and Danny Glover watch.

Chris Paul, Larry Fitzgerald, and "The Champ" with Dwayne Wade at a luncheon I organized honoring Dwayne in 1995.

Golf sensation Phil Michelson, who has won six major championships, was a big supporter of Celebrity Fight Night when he lived in Phoenix.

My Jewish friend Larry King often introduced me as his Christian friend and many times asked me questions about the Bible.

Jimmy Walker & Associates, Ltd.

5225 N. Central Avenue, Suite 106 / Post Office Box 7306 / Phoenix, Arizona 85011
(602) 230-1111 / Facsimile (602) 266-7820
9465 Wilshire Blvd. / Beverly Hills, CA 90212 / (213) 477-7500

November 2, 1989

Sam Walton
Wal Mart Stores
702 SW 8th St.
Bentonville, Ark. 72712

Dear Sam,

I'm happy to hear that Lucas' recent surgery was successful and according to
your helpful secretary, Becky, he is responding well following the operation.

Nancy and I, along with some of our friends including Pat Boone are praying for
your grandson and your family. Our only hope in this serious matter is our
trust in the Lord and we will continue to pray that little Lucas, through God's
healing, will receive a 100% recovery and return to excellent health.

We will continue to pray and please do not hesitate to give me a call if we may
be of any help.

Sincerely,

Jimmy Walker

JW:jat

Jimmy — Help us so much / Your concerns and prayers. Lucas is / Winning so far — Probably a year of radiation / and Chemo Therapy. But a fair chance of cure! / Thanks — so much —

Sam W.

Sam Walton was to retail what Michael Jordan was to basketball—the best.

Michael Jordan, Walter Davis, and me playing
golf at the Arizona Biltmore.

Fortunately, "The Champ" didn't break my jaw when he landed this punch.

Me with "The Champ" and David Foster

Not the greatest singing, but it was plenty of fun when
David Foster invited Michael Clarke Duncan, John Elway,
and Kareem Abdul-Jabbar to the stage to sing.

Reba McEntire has emceed Celebrity Fight Night for fifteen years, and David Foster has been our music director for twenty years. They deserve much credit for the success of CFN.

Me, Billy, and Janice Crystal visiting our good friend Muhammad Ali in his home.

Muhammad Ali was having fun with our grandchildren in our backyard.

Hanging with "The Big Fella" at a Suns game.

When Amar'e Stoudemire signed to play for the New York Knicks, I organized for him to meet fans at The Plaza hotel in New York. Kareem and Joe Cinque both attended.

Kevin Costner giving a toast to The Greatest of All Time—Muhammad Ali—after receiving the Muhammad Ali Humanitarian Award.

Steve Martin receiving an award from "The Champ"
with Billy Crystal enjoying the moment.

Lionel Richie and his good friend "The Champ" having some fun.

Jennifer Lopez throwing a serious punch at "The Champ."

Bob and Renee Parsons

Bruce and Diane Halle

Richard and Stacie Stephenson

Stephanie Argyros with her father and mother, George and Julia Argyros

Kelly Clarkson, Blake Shelton, and Reba McEntire

Superstar Kelly Clarkson asked a few girls to come up on the stage to sing with her. Would you believe almost 300 ladies rushed up on the stage!

Lynn and Foster Friess

Rita Wilson and Tom Hanks having a good time at our charity event.

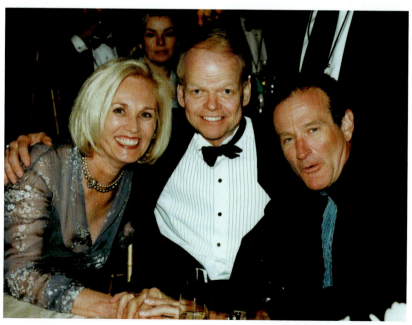

Robin Williams later stood on the chairs entertaining our guests. That had to be one of the most fun moments ever in Celebrity Fight Night history.

My daughters with their husbands, Jennifer and Ethan and Jon and Laurie

Harrison Ford being honored at Celebrity Fight Night.

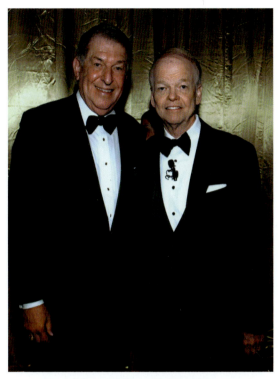

Me with Jerry Colangelo

Me with Walter Scott

Christine Jones with maybe the greatest women's basketball
player ever, Hall of Famer Nancy Lieberman.

I have been fortunate to have an excellent executive
director in Sean Currie at Celebrity Fight Night.

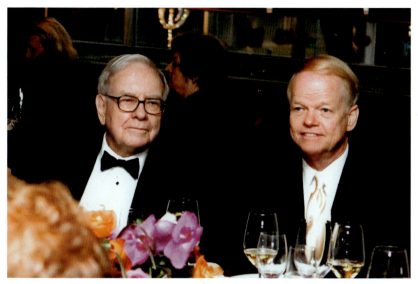

I was honored to sit next to Warren Buffett at a David Foster charity event in Calgary. He had a great sense of humor but, surprisingly, never asked me for any business advice.

I arrived early for our Celebrity Fight Night charity event at the historic Colosseum in Rome to make sure everything was well organized for an amazing night of entertainment.

Andrea Bocelli performed for Celebrity Fight Night and The Andrea Bocelli Foundation at the Colosseum in Rome.

Elton John performing at the Colosseum

Steven Tyler performing at the Colosseum

Me, Veronica, and Andrea Bocelli at a beach party in Italy

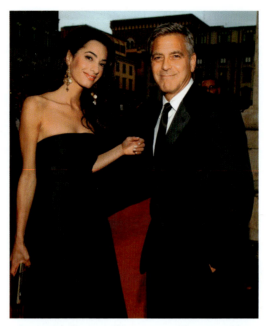

We honored George Clooney in Florence. He and his wife, Amal, have a home in Lake Como.

We honored Sophia Loren in Rome, where she lives.

Over 20,000 people in Florence, Italy, showed up to see celebrities for our Celebrity Fight Night at the historic Palazzo Vecchio, which was built in 1298.

I was honored at The Starkey Foundation in 2010 along with Forest Whitaker, Dennis Hansen, Richard Branson, and Ashton Kutcher, whose achievements far outshone mine.

Surprise bicycles in the tent for the Bicycles for
Kids Party benefitting inner-city children

Andrea Bocelli singing "Ave Maria" to the homeless at 7:00 a.m.
in 45-degree weather at the Phoenix St. Vincent de Paul.

It has been a privilege being a volunteer and speaking to, on average, about 500 homeless men and women at Never Give Up.

Reggie Jackson was Scott's favorite player as a little boy. The last insurance policy Scott sold several months before his passing was to "Mr. October."

The tennis court in our backyard with Bobby Riggs and Scott, age ten. Bobby won Wimbledon in 1941 and later lost to Billie Jean King in the "Battle of the Sexes" in 1973.

Scott, age eleven, in our backyard at a dinner party with his favorite basketball player—Michael Jordan.

Dad —

I had a good talk with mom last night and I am ready to really dedicate my life to Christ. We could all have so much fun together plus I could have the strength to sleep in my room. Tomorrow I will get my behavior report and we are going to go to Camelback Bible. John is Going to spend the night tonight because I know you like him. You are going to see some major changes in my life.

I LOVE YOU

P.S. wake me at 7:30 AM for my shower!

A note Scott wrote to me when he was fourteen

Scott caddying for me at the Phoenix Open Pro Am. Scott often would say, "Dad, why did you hit that shot?"

Dad –

I love you. Sorry I was in a bad mood last night. I hope you have a great trip to L.A. I will be praying for you, as always. You have taught me a lot about good + ethical business and I am impressed with your marketing and optimistic about yours, Jim's and my future. In the future, I will try to absorb your strengths, and improve upon, but not criticize either of our weaknesses. Thanks for being such a great Dad and setting such an outstanding example. I love you and mom very very much.

Love
Scott

P.S. – I like how we both want the ball in our hands! (you made me into this competitor)

A letter Scott wrote to me when he was twenty-seven years old

Scott and his mother, whom he loved, at a Cardinals game

lap as he drove a tractor in Williams, Iowa. We would gather eggs and throw them against his dad's barn and at the sows. Then we would throw corn cobs at each other. Al was a power forward on his basketball team at Williams High, where there were only seven seniors in his graduating class—and just 250 people in the entire town.

Al was our announcer for the first three years. He always began the event with his own version of "Let's Get Ready to Rumble!" He was great, as always.

Fight Night was a Suns-centric event. Colangelo brought most of his big-name players and personnel to the event. One of them was center Oliver Miller, who had a back injury and had not played a game in about a month. He was really enjoying the boxing competition between Barkley and Carbajal, and Barkley used that enthusiasm to his advantage.

"Hey, Oliver!" Barkley screamed. "Get up here and put Michael Carbajal on your shoulders. He's too small, and I want to hit him hard!"

With a bad back, Miller jumped into the ring. He put the five foot five Carbajal on his shoulders, and Barkley started punching him. The crowd loved it—except for the guys at my table.

I was seated next to Colangelo and former Suns head coach Cotton Fitzsimmons. They could not believe what they were seeing from Miller, a player who had not played a game in four weeks. Now he was in a boxing match, carrying a guy on his shoulders? I felt like I caused that problem.

But we all knew the deal: You could not stop Barkley once he got started. It was pointless to even try. And people just loved him. To this day, nobody can make me laugh faster than Charles.

People went to Suns games just to see Barkley. They did not care who won or lost. They just wanted to watch Charles Barkley. He could draw a crowd at a car wash. He was a superstar, and we caught him at the height of his powers.

When our inaugural Celebrity Fight Night had come to a close, we had raised $100,000. We exceeded six figures in our very first at-bat. We gave $60,000 of that total to Carbajal's boxing gym in Phoenix, helping a local institution stay afloat.

Colangelo said:

I rib Jimmy about the fact that he knew about networking before networking knew about itself. He somehow, whether it's instinctive or not, is an incredible communicator. Once he meets an individual, he is locked in. He did all of this before technology.

He is as good a communicator as you'll ever find. His philosophy on relationships is to stay in touch. Once he meets an individual, he gets to know birthdays and anniversaries and details about children, and he uses all of that in a very positive way.

It really impresses people. There are times you'll get a call or an email or a text out of the blue, or something very specific that's happening in the moment. He spends a considerable part of his day just staying in touch. It's a remarkable trait.

We expanded our minds and our menu. I used those floor seats of mine to recruit more famous people to Celebrity Fight Night. We had boxing icon Sugar Ray Leonard fight Dodgers manager Tommy Lasorda. We had quarterback Jake Plummer fight rock star Alice Cooper.

I once took Plummer to a Suns game on a recruiting trip for Celebrity Fight Night. The Suns were down by eighteen points with ninety seconds left in the game. I told Jake it was a good time to leave and beat the traffic.

He spun around and looked at me.

"Jimmy, we are not going anywhere!" Plummer said. "There are two people in this arena who know it is not over. [Suns point guard] Jason Kidd and myself!"

I took Alice Cooper golfing in hopes of recruiting him to Celebrity Fight Night. Every time I left a putt short of the hole, I heard exactly what you would expect from a rock-and-roll icon.

"Hit the ball, Alice," he would say.

I once had a golf outing lined up at the Raven Golf Club in South Phoenix, and I decided to invite Plummer as part of our foursome. The popular quarterback told me he was too busy that morning and that he needed to lift weights.

"Jake, are you sure you can't play golf?" I asked.

"No, I really can't. Maybe next week?" he responded.

"Well, that's too bad because Billy Crystal is coming," I said.

"You know, Jimmy, I think I can adjust my schedule and meet you for golf!" Plummer said.

We had a good laugh over that exchange, and I still needle him to this day about his quick change of heart.

I also recruited Major League Baseball star Greg Maddux over many rounds on the golf course. I never saw him miss a ten-foot putt. His command was incredible, on the greens and the pitching mound. He was just a natural.

We had Phil Mickelson box Billy Mayfair, a pair of PGA Tour stars who played collegiate golf at Arizona State University. We had Kidd take on NFL defensive star Simeon Rice. We donated money to the swim club run by the family of Gary Hall Jr., a famed Phoenix swimmer who won ten Olympic medals. Hall Jr. famously showed up for a race at the 2004 Athens Olympics wearing boxing shorts and a patriotic robe. Maybe his outfit was inspired by Celebrity Fight Night.

We pitted Super Bowl MVP Joe Montana against Verne Troyer, who famously played Mini-Me in the *Austin Powers* movies. Montana and Troyer came up with their own skit. Troyer stood two foot eight. He was going to wind up and hit Montana below the belt. In an exaggerated response, Montana was going to fall like a redwood in the forest, and Troyer was going to claim a knockout victory over one of the greatest quarterbacks in NFL history.

Then Troyer would take the microphone and announce, "I want a real fighter!"

Then boxing great Evander Holyfield would suddenly appear from nowhere, delighting the crowd.

It was time of great creativity at Celebrity Fight Night. We even experimented with an officially sanctioned boxing match between two real middleweights. But the violence was far too much for our audience. I distinctly remember some attendees leaving the ballroom when they saw blood streaming down the face of a real boxer. They retreated to the lobby for high tea.

None of this would have happened without Charles Barkley's participation, his good nature, his sense of community, and his great heart.

Barkley once said, "Jimmy is a wonderful person. He's never asked me for anything other than Celebrity Fight Night. He has no agenda. And this is going all the way back to 1994. It was a great thing to do. I'm happy for him and where he's taken Celebrity Fight Night. I'll take a little credit. But it's mostly a credit to him."

In our second year of Celebrity Fight Night, we took a big detour and delivered high-end musical entertainment. We had famed hitmaker Barry Manilow sitting at a piano inside the boxing ring when guests walked into our event. They were stunned!

Barry was in his prime. His business manager, Lester Knispel, was a friend of mine. We also brought in Paula Abdul to perform at that event. The crowd was goofy that night. At one point, Barry stopped playing and said, "If you're not going to be quiet, I'm not going to keep singing!" Afterward, Manilow said he loved the experience and had never performed before such an intimate gathering.

It was also crazy stuff because we did not tell our audience that Manilow and Abdul would be headlining Celebrity Fight Night as performing artists. They walked in for a celebrity boxing match and said, "Can you believe this?"

What they didn't know was I had an even bigger surprise up my sleeve.

CHAPTER 7

THE GREATEST OF ALL TIME

My Friendship with Muhammad Ali

I MET MUHAMMAD ALI IN 1985. HE WAS HAVING DINNER WITH Sammy Davis Jr. and Dr. Jerry Buss at the Forum Club in Los Angeles. They motioned for me to come over.

I was ready.

"Champ, we have a mutual friend in Earnie Shavers," I told Ali.

To my surprise, Ali said nothing.

I repeated my words.

Again, nothing.

Surely, Ali couldn't forget Shavers, the heavyweight he battled for fifteen rounds in 1977? One of the heaviest hitters in the history of the sport? The man who fought Ali the finish in Ali's last successful title defense?

Ali continued to stare.

I tried one last time.

"Champ, Earnie really loves you," I said.

"If he loved me so much, why did he hit me so hard?" Ali responded.

Thus began my unlikely, unbelievable, life-changing relationship with the greatest heavyweight fighter in boxing history. And let me tell you, he was as good as advertised.

Ali was the greatest.

As an athlete, he was ahead of his time. As a world-class boxer, he had dazzling hand speed and footwork. He was also an entertainer, a pioneer, and a promoter. He was young, handsome, eloquent, boastful, prideful, witty, charming, and full of real courage. When he spoke in rhymes, he sounded like a modern-day rapper. He loved being the center of attention—which was good, because you couldn't take your eyes off of him.

Ali invented the art of trash talking, and he loved to play pranks on unwitting people. He liked to tell me, "Jimmy, you're not as ugly as you look."

He said a lot of other things, too, but I can't put them in print.

Ali also stood up for social change. He stood firm against the Vietnam War and stared down prison time for refusing to fight for his country. He became a hero to one side of the country, and he was scorned by the other half of the political spectrum. He was an Olympic hero who joined the Nation of Islam and changed his name from Cassius Clay to Muhammad Ali, igniting a new era of black pride.

It was quite a ride.

Four years after winning a gold medal at the Rome Olympics in 1960, Ali became heavyweight champion of the world. Three years after that, he was convicted of draft evasion and banned from boxing for three years.

Our country eventually realized we should not be fighting that war. But it cost Ali almost four years of his prime.

Inside the ring, his courage and resiliency were legendary. Those traits also might have been his downfall. Ali waged epic battles against dangerous opponents like Joe Frazier, George Foreman, Sonny Liston, and Ken Norton. It's no big leap to believe the cumulative head trauma Ali absorbed during his career had something to do with the Parkinson's disease that muzzled the greatest communicator in sports history.

It was tragic and heartbreaking, but I'm sure he'd do it all over again.

Sometimes I think about if Ali had been born decades later, in a much smaller world connected by the Internet and fueled by social media. Imagine Ali on Twitter, trolling critics and opponents alike. That would've been a lot of fun.

There were times when I'd pick him up for an appointment or an appearance, and I'd be driving down the road. I'd glance to my right and feel the need to pinch myself. That's Muhammad Ali—the greatest of all time—sitting right next to me.

Sometimes while driving, I'd be focusing on the road and not paying attention to him at all. That's when he would stick a finger in my ear just to mess with me. Or he would pretend to be asleep and snoring, only to shock me when I tried to wake him up. He was funny like that.

My relationship with The Champ blossomed after our third Celebrity Fight Night, when I received word that Ali was in Phoenix receiving treatment for Parkinson's disease.

I had an epiphany. Partnering with Ali could turn our charity fundraiser into a world-class event. In return, we could create a charitable arm that would directly benefit Ali, his legacy, and those afflicted with Parkinson's disease.

I contacted Ali's wife, Lonnie. She was very open to the idea. I told her we could even name a Parkinson's Center after Ali.

She put me in touch with Dr. Abe Lieberman, who was in charge of Ali's treatment. Dr. Lieberman is famous for his excellent reputation in understanding Parkinson's disease. The rest is history.

Since 1994, we've given away almost $100 million to charities, most of which goes to the Muhammad Ali Parkinson Center at Barrow Neurological Institute in Phoenix. Money has also been distributed to numerous other charities.

Ali had a profound effect on Celebrity Fight Night. He drove the entire event. He was an irresistible lure that brought star-studded celebrities to our event. He was bigger than life, a living piece of history, an icon known all over the globe.

My journey with Ali is also deeply personal.

I am blessed to have shared quality time with Ali. Not because of his fame and his celebrity, but for the respect, compassion, patience, and kindness that he showed to everyone: the poor, the rich, and the sick. And especially to children.

Ali once discovered some of the patients at his Parkinson Center were not receiving their treatments because they had no way of getting to the hospital and no money for public transportation. Ali started sending money to be used for their cab fare, just so they would receive their Parkinson's medication.

When he told me about this, we directed some of the event proceeds to purchase a van with a hydraulic lift, which transported passengers to the Muhammad Ali Parkinson Center.

During our friendship, I took Ali to over twenty Suns games where we sat on the floor. Every time he walked in, he received a standing ovation from over 16,000 fans. He'd shadow box on the way to our seats, and they'd cheer even louder. Members of both teams would come over to pay homage. They couldn't believe they were meeting Ali. When that was over, Ali would motion for fans to come down and see him. He loved to interact with people.

When the game began, half the crowd would remain focused on Ali, which was just the way he liked it.

Ali was a master of practical jokes. When I'd pick him up at his house, he'd always want to bring his fart toy with us to Suns games. His wonderful wife, Lonnie, would say, "Now, Muhammad, you're not taking that."

He'd wait until she wasn't looking and stuff the fart toy in his pocket. Inside the arena, he'd squeeze it for sound effects at really awkward times. His face would get all serious, and he would look around like, "Who did that?"

One time, we were leaving a Mariners spring training game in Arizona and Ali rolled down the window. He put his head out for the world to see. People started going crazy, honking their horns all around us. Ali motioned for several vehicles to follow us, creating an impromptu convoy. Six carloads full of complete strangers actually followed us back to Ali's home.

Lonnie couldn't believe what she was seeing. She said, "Muhammad, who are these people?" He said they were his friends. She had to remind him that not everyone had his best interests in mind.

Sometimes when we would leave a Suns game, he would notice thick crowds waiting outside the team's parking garage. He would reach over and grab the wheel. That was the sign that he wanted me to stop. Then he would get out of the car and sign autographs for forty-five minutes. I didn't always care for that—not when I had to get home so I could get up and get to work the next morning.

One time after a game, Muhammad told me he was hungry. I said I'd call around and see what was open. Ali also told me not to mention his name. So I called Mark Tarbell, an elite chef and restaurateur in Arizona.

He told me his restaurant was just about to close.

"Keep your restaurant open," I said. "I've got somebody with me. It'll be worth your time. Trust me."

I arrived with Ali. He ordered three cheeseburgers. Except they came to the table with bacon, and Muslims don't eat pork. I ended up eating Ali's meal while he drew pictures on the tablecloth.

The Champ loved to go to novelty shops and magic stores. He loved to purchase handshake buzzers and packs of fake money. He was notorious for passing out trillion-dollar bills in restaurants.

As his disease progressed, Ali never complained and was rarely in a bad mood. When I could tell The Champ was a little off, I'd pull out my phone and call Billy Crystal. Billy knew how to make him laugh. He'd imitate Ali and famed broadcaster Howard Cosell. That always brought a smile to Ali's face.

The Champ loved to watch *Rocky* movies. He also loved Michael Phelps, the Olympic swimmer who rose to stardom at the 2008 Beijing Olympics. Those were the first Olympics televised in high definition, and, like most of us, Ali was riveted to the swimming competition. He would stay up to all hours of the night watching Phelps swim his races.

Other times, I would arrive at his house and The Champ would be watching films of his old fights...especially the ones with Frazier.

Ali vs. Frazier remains among the gold standards for sports rivalries. Like the Yankees vs. Red Sox or Lakers vs. Celtics.

Ali and Frazier fought forty-one rounds over three different bouts from 1971–75. Neither man was the same after the trilogy concluded. Ali was hit with Parkinson's disease, and Frazier had slurred speech. They damaged each other badly.

Ali also knew how to get in his head.

Before one of their fights in Manila, the capital city of the Philippines, Ali mercilessly ridiculed Frazier. It included one of his most infamous sound bites.

"It will be a chiller, a killer, and a thriller when I get the gorilla in Manila!" Ali said.

Then he reached into his pocket, pulled out a black rubber gorilla, and began punching the toy animal.

"This is the way Joe Frazier looks when you hit him," Ali said. "Joe is so ugly, his mother told me that when he was a little boy, every time he cried, the tears would stop, turn around, and go down the back of his head!"

Ali was only trying to promote the fight. He was trying to entertain the audience and make people laugh. But Frazier could never see past the hurt to what Ali was trying to do. He couldn't see all the money Ali had made for them both with all that trash talking. And he carried a heavy grudge.

While Ali bravely displayed his disease to the world, lighting the Olympic cauldron with a shaking hand at the Opening Ceremonies in Atlanta 1996, Frazier wasn't impressed. He staged an unscheduled press gathering at the Olympic boxing venue in the following days, claiming that Ali deserved his disease, that somehow God had punished him.

It was a shame because Ali was nothing like the picture that Frazier painted. For all his comical boasts, Ali never once believed he was more important than anyone else. That's incredibly rare among someone of his celebrity status. And I would know. I've spent most of my life around celebrities.

Once, I did a favor for Bruce Halle, a friend of mine and the CEO of Discount Tire. I brought Ali to corporate headquarters so he could make an appearance in front of Halle's employees. Ali stretched our thirty-minute visit into a full two hours, signing autographs and taking pictures with everyone in the building.

Ali liked to say, "The greatest religion in the world is the religion of love." Ali had love—maybe not in the ring when he was bashing people's brains in—but he had love.

CHAPTER 8

THE GOLDEN TICKET

The Influence of Ali

I WASN'T PLANNING ON MEETING WORLD-RENOWNED OPERA singer Andrea Bocelli at The Ritz-Carlton hotel in New York.

I was in the lobby of the hotel with Jerry Colangelo when he noticed Bocelli waiting by the bank of elevators.

Colangelo retold the story from that day. "That's Andrea Bocel—," I said. "And before I could finish the sentence, Jimmy had already bee-lined over there."

Bocelli is blind. Otherwise, he would've seen me stick my arm between the elevators doors just before they closed.

I quickly told Bocelli we had a mutual friend in songwriter David Foster, who provided the music for Celebrity Fight Night. I explained how the event raises money for the Muhammad Ali Parkinson Center.

As soon as he heard Ali's name, Bocelli's face lit up.

"Muhammad Ali is my hero!" Bocelli said. "I love Muhammad! Do you know Muhammad Ali?"

"Yes, he is my friend," I said.

Quick on my feet, I remembered that Bocelli was performing in Phoenix the following week.

"Andrea," I said. "If Muhammad is in town when you come to Arizona, we could go to his house in Scottsdale and I would be happy to introduce you."

Bocelli was beyond excitement. He nearly lost it.

"You could introduce me to Muhammad Ali?" he said. "I would love to meet him!"

All of that happened in the span of one elevator ride. It was magic.

Later, I called Lonnie for clearance.

"Absolutely," she said. "Muhammad loves Bocelli's music."

Done.

The following week, Nancy and I met Bocelli, his future wife, Veronica, and his manager, Carlo Tomba, at the Phoenix Ritz-Carlton. It was also Lonnie's birthday, so I brought along a cake. I also brought along a couple of close friends, famous author and businessman Harvey Mackay and his wife, Carol Ann. This was around Christmas, so a friend gave us hats that resembled reindeer antlers. We all put them on. Because Ali loved the goofy stuff.

We rang the doorbell. Lonnie was overwhelmed when Bocelli started singing "Happy Birthday" to her while wearing Christmas antlers. And that was just the beginning.

I walked into a house with a famous man who is blind and introduced him to a famous man who had almost completely lost his voice to Parkinson's disease. That in and of itself was a challenge.

Bocelli immediately embraced Ali. He kissed him on both cheeks. And then he got down on his knees, supplicating himself to The Champ.

"Muhammad, I am humbled and honored and privileged to be next to you in your home," Bocelli said. "I am very nervous. I want you to know you have been my hero all my life."

Bocelli stood up, hugged Ali again, planting even more kisses on his cheeks. And that's when Ali's voice emerged from his mouth, breaking down all the obstacles along the way.

"Will you sing to me?" he asked Bocelli.

My mouth fell open. I hadn't heard Ali speak that clearly in a long time.

Bocelli couldn't wait to oblige. He sang a song from an Italian opera on the spot in Ali's family room. Tears were shed. We all had goose bumps.

Bocelli invited us to his concert the following evening. In front of 18,000 people at Jobing.com Arena in Glendale, he walked onstage with boxing gloves on his hands. He told the audience his dream had come true. He had met his hero, Muhammad Ali.

After the concert, Bocelli met up with us backstage. He gave Ali another long hug. Then he told me he wanted to return the favor.

"What can I do to help The Champ's charity?" he asked.

Bocelli would eventually perform at Celebrity Fight Night in Phoenix. During the live auction, he agreed to have dinner with one of our donors, and the winning bid was $260,000. The following year, a private dinner at his home in Tuscany sold for $300,000.

Bocelli was also instrumental in helping us stage the first international Celebrity Fight Night, where guests paid $60,000 per person for an event in Tuscany, Italy, arriving courtesy of Mark Cuban's private jet. That year, Bocelli performed with Lionel Richie and John Legend.

Bottom line: If I had not gone and stuck my arm inside that elevator, I would've never met Bocelli. We would have never raised that kind of money for the Muhammad Ali Parkinson Center.

It felt like destiny.

Andrea Bocelli recounted the story:

An elevator that is ready to go up. Jimmy is there, in my memory, behind the sliding doors of the cabin while they are going to close. I go up and down, in the hotel that overlooks Central Park, as if it were my second home. On the top floor, there is my refuge in New York, a muffled place to rest and study. It seems to be on the peak of a forest but, on the contrary, it is in the heart, or even better, the navel of the world.

The elevator is going to go up, behind it there is Jimmy. I do not remember a handshake. But his hand that chooses to slip, at its own risk, between the doors and thus stops the closing in extremis. He enters between me and Veronica, a sudden and unexpected colleague in our rise. Taking advantage of the forced intimacy and without wasting time, he does not turn out to be a robber. He does not want our wallets. But he is asking for a confirmation of his suppositions: "Are you Bocelli?"

After expressing his strong admiration for the results of my profession, he told us he was a friend and a cooperator of Muhammad Ali. A few minutes later, after breaking the ice, we got aware of the happy circumstance that would take me, in the following days, just to Phoenix for a concert.

Jimmy is many things: self-sacrifice, generosity, solidarity, and friendship. But if I had to speak of him in a flash, I would choose the image of a hand, his, forcing the hand of fate opening the door of that elevator, almost closed, thus giving birth to a beautiful friendship and giving me the possibility to meet his friend and the legend of two, maybe three generations, therefore even mine since the days of my early childhood: Muhammad Ali.

Everybody felt that way about Ali. He was a powerful magnet to the stars. His presence drew eight Super Bowl MVPs to Celebrity Fight Night. He drew Willie Mays, one of the greatest players in Major League Baseball history; Wayne Gretzky, the greatest hockey player ever born; Kareem Abdul-Jabbar, one of the greatest players in NBA history; Michael Phelps, the transcendent swimmer who won twenty-three Olympic gold medals; Jack Nicklaus, the golfer with the most grand slam titles in PGA Tour history; PGA star Phil Mickelson; and NFL star Larry Fitzgerald, just to name a few.

Ali was the Pied Piper. He inspired reverence and humility from all other celebrities. We would typically average abound forty sports and entertainment celebrities every year, and Ali turned them all into giddy fans. He made A-list celebrities feel the kind of idol worship that most Americans felt for them. Ali was the one they all wanted to meet. Here is what a few of those stars had to say about Ali:

Mary Lou Retton, Olympian: "I come because it's Ali, man. You know, he does that whole butterfly thing and he's awesome. You just hear 'Ali' and it's like a magnet. We flock to him because we just admire him so much."

Alice Cooper, iconic rock star: "Ali is the most recognized person on the planet. I, like everybody, lived and died with every fight he had. I see my whole life sitting there with Muhammad Ali."

Céline Dion: "Performing in front of The Champ at Fight Night was such a great thrill for me. I felt his energy, and it was something I'll remember forever."

We never failed to sell out once Ali began headlining our event. Our bullpen of A-list stars increased dramatically.

We can start with Billy Crystal, whom I met in the late 1980s. Crystal was a Clippers' season-ticket holder. I met him through my association with team owner Donald Sterling, an insurance client of mine.

I once asked Crystal why he didn't cheer for the Lakers, a team that has produced superstars, championship banners, and statutes outside the arena.

"Jimmy, you don't understand," he said. "I'm from New York. The Clippers are my kind of team. I'm a grassroots guy."

It didn't take me long to realize that Crystal was also a huge fan of Ali. His impression of Ali was considered the best in the industry. His first standup act in comedy was based on his interpretation of Ali.

David Foster, a songwriter and sixteen-time Grammy Award winner, became our entertainment coordinator. I met the iconic Foster at the Grammys. He also signed up because of Ali, beginning a streak of twenty-five consecutive appearances at Celebrity Fight Night.

I agreed to pay $25,000 to Foster's foundation, and he was very appreciative. He did such a good job that we gave his foundation $50,000 instead. He signed on the following year for $50,000 and was so good in his encore performance that we wrote a check for $100,000. Today Foster remains a close friend.

Foster once asked me if we could invite an eighteen-year-old singer named Josh Groban to our smaller event on Friday, the day that precedes Celebrity Fight Night. I told David I had never heard of Josh Groban.

"Don't worry, Jimmy," Foster told me. "He will be a big star someday."

The following year, Foster had a similar request. He asked me if he could invite a twenty-year-old singer named Michael Bublé. I told him I had never heard of Michael Bublé, but David said, "Don't worry. He will be a big star someday."

I'm glad I listened, as both have become superstars and frequent headline performers at Celebrity Fight Night. And you won't find two nicer guys in the entertainment profession.

Rod Stewart performed at Celebrity Fight Night because of Ali, a partnership that included memorable negotiations between me and Stewart's agent, Arnold Stiefel.

I met Stiefel at his Beverly Hills home. Our meeting was scheduled for 11:00 a.m. He showed up at the front door in his bathrobe and pajamas.

Stiefel had a huge dog named Claire. I remember sitting on a couch in his living room when Claire jumped on top of me. The dog must've weight 200 pounds.

I immediately told Stiefel that Claire was my father's name. We found that quite amusing.

Five minutes later, I noticed I was covered in dog hair. Claire had shed all over my black suit. But the dog wouldn't stop. It kept panting and huffing and licking and salivating. The dog nuzzled me so much that Stiefel was taken aback.

"You really like my dog, don't you?" he said.

"Absolutely," I lied. "I love your dog. Such a beautiful animal."

Convincing Stiefel of my love for his dog helped land Rod Stewart as headline performer at Celebrity Fight Night—even though I left his home covered in dog hair, dripping in drool, and wearing shoes that were badly scratched by the dog's long nails.

Years later, I shared this story with music legend Clive Davis, who told me that Stiefel's dog had just passed away. He also told me that Stiefel replaced Claire with another dog that he named Pearl.

My dad's name was Claire. My mom's name was Pearl. And those where the last two pet names chosen by a guy I was recruiting to land Rod Stewart. What are the odds of that?

Davis and I immediately conferenced Stiefel into our telephone call and we all laughed for ten minutes.

One year at Celebrity Fight Night, we honored actress Halle Berry.

"Oh my gosh, I'm so honored to get this award," she said. "I just thought of something. I married all of these other men. I should have married Muhammad."

With perfect comedic timing, Lonnie Ali responded, "Here he is. He's all yours. You can take him."

Once I took NBA star Chris Paul to meet Ali at his favorite Scottsdale diner. On the way back, Paul appeared overwhelmed by the experience. He said it was one of the greatest days of his life.

Once Céline Dion was onstage singing at Celebrity Fight Night when she abruptly stopped in the middle of the song. She made her musicians stop playing. The room went silent. She addressed her husband, René Angélil. "René, do you know who you're sitting next to? You're sitting next to Muhammad Ali, the greatest of all time!"

In 2005, we honored actor Michael J. Fox, who was also battling Parkinson's disease.

"I'm happy to be in the same corner as Muhammad Ali," Fox said.

And once, Lakers great Magic Johnson said these unforgettable words to The Champ at Celebrity Fight Night: "If it wasn't for you, I couldn't be Magic."

Rap mogul Puff Daddy badly wanted to meet Ali. When I met up with the artist, also known as Sean Combs, he had an entourage of about six Cadillac Escalades. We pulled into Ali's neighborhood and the security detail was so paranoid they actually checked out the backyards of Ali's neighbors.

Still, the most stirring tribute to Ali came from the mouth of actor Kevin Costner, who delivered a powerful speech to the Celebrity Fight Night audience in 2015.

Here's how he described his speech:

You are asked to go to these chicken dinners, and this one is the top of the heap, so you want to be respectable. I had heard of Fight Night, and Jimmy has a way about him. He called and asked if I'd do this. It's not my favorite thing to speak (in public). I know it's about raising money. I had a hard time doing a speech about myself, "Thank you, I've worked hard, blah blah blah." I felt that wasn't where I wanted to go. Why not talk about Ali, the reason we're gathered?

I'm glad I did. I labored over the speech for two weeks. It didn't come easy. I went back to my youth when he popped on the scene. I talked about The Champ, not myself. The speech was the story.

When I first heard of him, my dad hated him. I watched him through my career, through the Vietnam War. My dad fought in that. I was encouraged at every turn not to like him. Public opinion turned in his favor. I really wanted to honor him and not pull any punches. After the speech four or five guys from the Islam religion came up to me. They were surprised and congratulated me for identifying Ali in a way they'd never heard before. But I did labor over that. I'm glad it had a level of meaning. The family immediately came to me and asked if they could have the speech [for the Muhammad Ali Center in Louisville, Kentucky].

Here is the text of Costner's incredible speech, which he delivered with Lonnie and Muhammad seated on stage right next to him. It is a poignant and profound tribute to the greatest of all time, and the practical joker who occasionally liked to put his finger in my ear:

Muhammad Ali is not just a man's name. To my mind, it has become more than that. It has become an idea, a state of mind. It evokes awe and admiration. It has become legend. To those of us who were lucky enough to see him in action both in and out of the ring, we know something that others don't, and may not be able to fully appreciate. Like trying to imagine Edmund Hillary climbing Mount Everest; Charles Lindberg flying solo across the Atlantic; when our young president challenged the nation to ask not what our country could do for us but what we could do for our country.

Muhammad Ali did things that will live in the hearts and minds of people forever. He changed our lives and not just because he was the greatest boxer who ever lived. He was. And not because he was beautiful ... I guess. But because more than any other person in sports history, he represented to me the effect a champion can have on the world when they leave their sport.

My first memory of Muhammad Ali came from my father. I was listening to him talk to another man about a boxing match that was going to happen that night. Even though I was only eight years old, I could tell from his voice that he did not think much of you. He did not think much of your chances. Words like, "arrogant, lack of respect, hadn't paid your dues." I even think I heard him say, "He ain't no Joe Louis."

I didn't know who Joe Louis was, either. But I could tell that my dad was sure that some guy named Sonny Liston was going to fix everything. So together, in the dark, my father and I listened to the radio. I remember sitting his lap. Two profound things happened that night:

The first was you did shake up the world, my friend, and it would never be the same. The second was that I realized my dad, my own hero, could be absolutely wrong about something he was absolutely sure of. My dad was mad. He thought Liston was a bum and he must've given up. I was secretly glad. And I agreed with you, that you probably were the greatest. I wanted to know more about you, bad manners and all.

You were not an easy person to root for in my house. I kept thinking why couldn't you be more quiet? Why couldn't you seem to have just a little more humility in victory? Even I could see their point. So I decided that I would try to be humble for you. And just when we were both starting to make a little progress, you and the world, me and my pop, you went and changed your name. You changed your religion. And you refused to fight in a war in Vietnam against a people with whom you had no quarrel. The '60s were a confusing time, and no one was more confusing to white America than you.

Those who first doubted your boxing abilities and were proved to be wrong switched their attack. Now they questioned your patriotism, your courage, your unwillingness to fight outside the ring. It was a predictable response. It was convenient. And it was lazy, an uninformed view of your dramatic personal stance. And overnight you became Public Enemy No. 1.

Looking at you tonight, I'm sure you feel the love in the room. But if we put your life in reverse, we would see how you suffered and we would see that you were all alone, armed only with a conviction of your faith. You took it from all sides. It was unfair. If it was a fight, somebody would've stopped it. Somebody should've. Somebody should've thrown the flag for piling on. And just like the greatest screen heroes, you never blamed or explained. You never said a word. With everything on the line—your reputation, the best years of your boxing life, your own personal freedom. You stood dead center in the middle of the ring and refused to turn your back on your principles and your religion. You broke with the conventional wisdom of the time, and you were right. Everybody was wrong about Vietnam. You never surrendered in the ring and you never surrendered outside it. Your title was taken away from you. You were robbed. But in doing so, you won the greatest battle of all. You won the love of the people.

Women, men, poor people, rich people, white people, black people, children . . . you become the most famous person in the world putting on a show. I can remember you quickly combing your hair waiting for a decision. What were you doing? I mean, who does that? Who does that at such a moment?

You were a sly one, Muhammad, and we know now you were fixing yourself up to play a greater role than just a boxer we all saw. You became the most famous person in the world pretending to be a fighter when you were really a man of peace.

When you came back to us, you were almost the same. The old battle lines were redrawn, but something was different. A shift was occurring in the country, and now when you went down, we ached. Those who thought they wanted it most now unexplainably found themselves standing with the rest of us, cheering. Willing you to get up. A shift was occurring in the country. A shift was occurring because you never did. And suddenly we knew that a man like you was once in a lifetime.

Thank you for taking us on your extraordinary journey. For the fleeing moments when we all thought we could float like a butterfly. Thank you for the amazing nights under the lights when you stung like a bee. Without bitterness, you let us mere mortals be great with you. You allowed us to be courageous. You allowed us to do the impossible. When you fought Joe Frazier in the Thrilla in Manila we couldn't have gotten off our chair, in our corner. But you did. Somehow you got up when we couldn't.

And when George Foreman was staggered in Africa, it seemed like the impossible was happening. We were afraid he would hurt you and humiliate you that night. We didn't want to see you beaten and on your knees. We didn't expect you to win. Because we couldn't have. But you did. You covered up and you took a beating. You took a beating until there was no fight left in a man who had come to kill you. And when he fell down, it was like a mighty redwood had been toppled, It was like the *Titanic* going down. It was Goliath lying dead in a field and

David standing over him, a man of faith, a man who believed in himself and helped us believe in ourselves.

It's been said that only another man can make another man cry. I don't know many who didn't the night you stood at the top of [Atlanta's] Olympic Stadium. The world held its breath as you stood alone, unaided, holding a torch that you had been carrying for us all these years. You were the perfect man for that perfect moment.

I didn't weep that night because you were no longer thirty years old and in your prime. Or because your hands would not stop trembling. I wept because that night because two profound things happened again.

Without saying a word, standing in silent dignity, you shook up the world. My father and I were both watching again. The only difference is, this time I was too big for his knee. And he didn't speak for the longest time. And I didn't think to break the silence of that moment. Finally, he turned to me and he quietly said, "He is the greatest, son."

My life had come full circle that wondrous night with you, me, and my dad. It was an example to all of us that if we reach for the stars we might someday become one.

Wallace Stegner wrote a great novel of the Old West, *The Angle of Repose*. When asked what the title meant, he said it is the way that you are held in the hearts of those that knew you when you were alive.

So I offer up again that Muhammad Ali is not just a man's name. It's a prayer. It's a whisper. A chant. A rallying cry. A trumpet call. It's a challenge to be the best we can be. Muhammad Ali is not just a man's name. It's a magical place where men can triumph and be celebrated.

To that point, I wonder how many of us remember the movie *Spartacus*, when the Romans were asking the rebel slaves which among them is Spartacus. And if he will step forward, the rest will be spared. And so to save his men, he stands up as he says he is Spartacus. And then one by one, each of his men stands up and says that he is Spartacus.

Spartacus is not a man's name anymore, either. It has become a battle cry, a battle cry to free men everywhere. So tonight, I want to raise my glass, and I ask you to do the same.

To the first and greatest Muhammad Ali: It is the name of all good men everywhere who are fighting the good fight. Your fight has always been to make the world a better place. And you've won. We thank you for showing us how to be a warrior, and we thank you for showing us how to be a peaceful warrior. In our best moments, we are all Muhammad Ali.

Costner's speech received a standing ovation that lasted several minutes. The Champ was a big fan of Costner, just like everyone else in attendance at Celebrity Fight Night. To this day, people still tell me it is the greatest speech they have ever heard.

CHAPTER 9

CELEBRITY FIGHT NIGHT

A Legacy of Giving

CELEBRITY FIGHT NIGHT BECAME "THE BIG GAME" OF charity events. We attached Roman numerals to each year's gala. And just like "The Big Game," each of our events featured great performances, fantastic finishes, and memories that lasted a lifetime.

"It's like the Nobel Prizes with an open bar," the late, great Robin Williams said.

You want stories?

Our event producer, Lori McAllister, once politely asked Robin Williams to be clean and avoid profanity during his on-stage performance. Robin agreed, and then he started auctioning off a private dinner with him in San Francisco. But first Robin said he wanted to auction off his testicles.

The crowd could not stop laughing. He quickly changed the subject.

Earlier in the evening, Robin put together a three-on-three football game in the men's room at the Arizona Biltmore Resort. He told everyone that he was Joe Montana. My son, Scott, was one of his favorite receivers.

"Dad, I was catching passes from Robin Williams in the bathroom!" Scott told me incredulously. "He was using a roll of toilet paper as the football!"

Naturally, Robin claimed his team won and he had earned Most Valuable Player honors.

Country music superstar Reba McEntire is my dear friend. She has served as emcee at Celebrity Fight Night in Phoenix for fifteen consecutive years. I've always said Reba is one our three MVPs, along with Ali and Foster. The only thing that could stop her streak was a pandemic, which shut down the world and put us on temporary hiatus.

At Celebrity Fight Night XII, one donor paid $250,000 to have dinner with Reba.

Reba had a better idea.

"If we add Faith Hill and her husband, Tim McGraw, don't you think the value should go up?" Reba asked.

The donor smiled and said he'd be happy to double his offer, agreeing to pay $500,000.

At that moment, Garth Brooks grabbed the microphone.

"Reba is not that good of a cook and her house ain't that great!" Brooks said.

The audience went crazy.

The donor was an investment manager, and he ended up with a bargain.

"We also brought along Kelly Clarkson, Ron and Jeanine Dunn from Brooks & Dunn, and Bill Ingle," Reba said. "We had a blast. It was good old country cooking."

At Celebrity Fight Night XV, one donor and his wife bid $300,000 to have dinner with Reba. But the couple never got around to scheduling a date. They called our office and said they would just donate that money to our charity.

One evening, two very generous donors wanted to have dinner with Reba and engaged in a bidding war. Each paid $1 million to have dinner with the Queen of Country Music. Reba was speechless.

Another generous donor provided a dinner with Reba at Walter Scott's home in Omaha, Nebraska. The gathering also included Warren and Astrid Buffett, Melissa Peterman, Cindy Smith, and Gail Yanney. We had a fabulous time. Buffett carried the evening with his jokes. Reba even noted the multi-billionaire had a future in standup comedy if he ever needed the money.

We had honored Scott the previous year, and we looped in Buffett for the tribute video. Buffett began his tribute by trolling one of his closest friends.

"Do I know Walter Scott?" he asked, pretending not to know his friend.

* * * * *

Over the years, Reba has hosted over ten dinners at her home while raising over $3 million for Celebrity Fight Night. I can't say enough good things about her. She is one of our true champions. Here's what she had to say about her experiences at Celebrity Fight Night:

I've never been part of such a successful benefit. When I first went to Celebrity Fight Night, I thought this would be like all the others. But when I got there, I saw all these huge celebrities and sports figures. I looked around and wondered what made this benefit so different.

At first, I thought it was Muhammad Ali. And then I met Jimmy Walker. To see how Jimmy can connect to people is one of the greatest things I've ever seen. He's very charismatic. You know at once he's sincere. He has that feel about him. Some people you are leery about. You know, like, what's your angle? But Jimmy is so pure. I'm blown away by him. He's the greatest networking person I've ever met.

The first year I hosted, I walked up to the podium. People were talking and mingling and it's hard to get everybody in their seats. I stood at the podium trying to talk. Jim Carrey was being honored that night, and he started yelling at everybody. He stood up in his seat and yelled, "You all shut up! Don't you know who that is up there talking? That's Reba McEntire!"

Robin Williams was at the other end of the table. He stood up as well, blurting out a line of gibberish that ended with the words, "Reba McEntire!"

And then Jim said, "I want you to get in your seat and I want you to be quiet!"

Williams did the same thing, translating Carrey's messages into his own special language. They go back and forth. And when people finally worked their way into their seats, Jim says, "Take it away, Reba!"

I was spellbound. And flattered for them coming to my rescue. I had no control over that audience at all. Those two guys won my heart that night. I love them both.

Another time, Nancy [Walker] came up to me and asked if I wanted my picture taken with Shaquille O'Neal. We went to his table and he looked like a parent who had gone to the kindergarten room instead of a dinner table. I stood next to him and my head came to his armpit. I said, "Wait a minute!" I pulled out chair, and I had a dress on, and I climbed up on that chair and took a picture with him. It's still hanging in my house.

Jim Carrey said of the event, "The funny thing about coming to Celebrity Fight Night and giving your time or giving a little money, you end up leaving richer than when you came."

Some of the most memorable moments at our events throughout the years are seeing celebrities doing unique and special things on stage—things you would never see them do anywhere else. Much of that credit goes to our tremendous friend, David Foster. In addition, because of Gregg Ostro at GO Media, we have had excellent videos of almost all of our charity events from the beginning.

Foster has been our musical director of our event for two decades. He not only provides unparalleled validity to our musical production that comforts the entertainers who join us each year, but he creates special moments on stage among the celebrities. I'll never forget the time he got John Elway, Kareem Abdul-Jabbar, and the late Michael Clarke Duncan on stage together singing! I guarantee no one has ever seen that trio before! Foster makes our events special in these unique ways, like only he can.

When we reach out to A-list entertainers and ask them to perform at our event, as soon as they hear that Foster is directing our music, they immediately know that the entire production will be of the highest professional quality. They know they will always look and sound good. Foster brings a professional dedication to excellence that always shines on stage for our entertainers and our guests.

Plus, David Foster knows how to end a show! Throughout the years, he has created special moments where he brings all the entertainers back on stage to close the show with a fun and inspirational song. One year, he brought hundreds of women from our audience on the stage to sing along with Kelly Clarkson.

I also remember the chaos that caused with our security team. Their heads were spinning. Our producer was afraid of the worst-case scenario: What if the stage collapsed? With all those women on stage dancing and singing, who knows what might have happened?

Imagine the potential injuries and liability issues. I tried not to think about that.

Instead, what *did* happen was another memorable ending to an amazing Celebrity Fight Night—thanks to David Foster. Having an appreciated friend like him on your team makes a big difference in so many ways.

One time, I was on stage paying tribute to my wife, Nancy. I must have been laying it on really thick because Tom Hanks started making fun of me. He looked at Nancy and said, "Give me a shovel because it is getting deep around here. Is Jimmy in trouble or something?"

We've raised a ton of money over the years. Individual tickets sell for as much as $10,000. During Celebrity Fight Night XIII, dinner and a round of golf with the great Arnold Palmer at his club in Latrobe, Pennsylvania, went for $600,000!

On two separate occasions, donors paid $500,000 each to play a round of golf and have lunch with PGA Tour star Phil Mickelson in Rancho Santa Fe in California.

Over twenty-plus years, our top live auction bids have been:

A foursome of golf with Arnold Palmer, $600,000; dinner with Billy Crystal and Robin Williams, $525,000; dinner with Andrea Bocelli and a week in Tuscany, $525,000; dinner with Reba McEntire, Tim McGraw, and Faith Hill, $500,000; a foursome of golf with Phil Mickelson (twice), $500,000; dinner with Muhammad Ali, $400,000; dinner with Reba McEntire (five times) $3 million; and a one-of-a-kind Rausch Racing P51 Ford Mustang, $300,000.

Clearly, the event was a success, but the most exciting part was that the money went to help other people!

In 2014, actor and comedian Steve Martin had a very special announcement to make. "Tonight has raised more money than any previous year . . . had it not been for my fee," Martin joked.

The crowd loved that one. Ali even looked at him sideways.

Famed actor Robert De Niro was just as funny. He said, "The Champ had fifty-six wins, and thirty-seven by KO," De Niro said. "In *Raging Bull*, I had sixteen wins, not including reruns on the DVD."

We created an event with a great champion, a great cause, and a great energy that flowed through a roomful of diverse celebrities, all of whom melted in the presence of Ali.

We appreciated many country stars who have performed at Celebrity Fight Night in Phoenix and Italy. This list includes Reba McEntire, Carrie Underwood, Blake Shelton, Garth Brooks, Trisha Yearwood, Kelly Clarkson, Michael W. Smith, Kenny Rogers, Faith Hill, Miley Cyrus, Billy Ray Cyrus, and Lee Greenwood.

The results were unbelievable. Once we even received a $2 million donation from New York financier Stewart Rahr. Rahr said:

> You can attribute that to Jimmy Walker, and what motivates him. I love him as a human being and what he stands for. That's why so much money was given, why I gave an extra million. From the moment the event is over, he's already starting to figure out how he can raise more money for the following year by hooking up the celebrities and the entertainment. When I see a guy who is so dedicated to a cause, an altruistic cause to raise money to give away, something stays with me. When I had an opportunity to reciprocate, I felt this was the right thing to do for The Champ and for what the event stands for.
>
> "We make a living by what we get, but we make a life by what we give."
>
> I got that from Winston Churchill. It stuck with me.

At this point, I need to pay tribute to Billy Crystal. He has deeply impacted my life, mostly by the way he has handled his success. Billy and his wife, Janice, have been married for over four decades. Family values are most important to him. He taught me the importance of having a good sense of humor. He always finds something witty to say in most every situation. What he did for Celebrity Fight Night was really off the charts. He consistently auctioned off dinners that included Crystal and some rotation of his best friends: Steve Martin, Martin Short, and Jimmy Kimmel.

In 2013, Crystal was horrified by the impact Hurricane Sandy had on his hometown of Long Beach, New York. He reached out to Ali to see how we could help. We gave Billy a Celebrity Fight Night platform to solicit donations specifically targeted for recovery efforts in Long Beach, and we raised $888,000. Billy tossed in the rest and donated a whopping $1 million dollars to his hometown.

Billy called me in the late 1990s when he was filming *Forget Paris*. He won the lead role in a movie about an NBA referee. The NBA promised they would put him in touch with some of the league's younger players, but Billy was growing impatient. I connected him with some of my friends and clients in the NBA, who were happy to help Billy research his upcoming role.

At Celebrity Fight Night XIX, Andrea Bocelli and Jennifer Lopez both performed. It was a magical night, even though Jennifer split her pants while performing on stage. Bocelli told me afterwards that he wanted to expand our friendship and our partnership. He insisted we bring the event to Italy.

Just like that, Celebrity Fight Night in Italy was launched in 2014. We were an international phenomenon.

For twenty-five years, Celebrity Fight Night was more than just a great party, a red-carpet extravaganza that brought the world's biggest names to Arizona. It was substance and style. It ranked among the heavyweights of philanthropic events in America.

We never dreamed that our little charity event in 1994 would evolve into something like this.

Celebrity Fight Night is fortunate to have Sean Currie as our executive director. Currie has done an excellent job for the past twenty-three years. He has great leadership qualities and has earned the respect of everyone he works with and has a real passion to help charities. He always gives 110 percent and deserves much credit for the success of our Celebrity Fight Nights in Phoenix and in Italy.

The Celebrity Fight Night Foundation appreciates the special donations from Bob and Renee Parsons with their foundation; along with the Diane and Bruce Halle Foundation; Foster and Lynn Friess Foundation; Julia and George Argyros Foundation with Stephanie; Richard and Stacie Stephenson Foundation; the Walter Scott Foundation; and the Stewart Rahr Foundation, just to name a few for their extreme generosity.

Finally, I want to give a huge thanks to everyone who has supported our charity event throughout the years.

CHAPTER 10

BLOOPER REEL

Mistakes from the Big Stage

I T CAN GET CAN ROUGH INSIDE THE RING AT CELEBRITY FIGHT Night. Energy can spin out of control. So can expectations and desires among A-list celebrities who expect to get what they want at all times.

It is an easy job until you try to do it well.

As evangelist/publisher Dwight L. Moody once said, "If you can't learn from your mistakes then don't make any."

I thought it would be fun to share some of my biggest blunders:

1. Denying Tom Brady. The most-decorated quarterback in NFL history came to our event early in his career, maybe after his second year in the league. I hooked him up with a golf outing in Arizona, and he appreciated that. He also absolutely loved meeting Muhammad Ali. We were off to a good start.

The following year, Tom wanted to return to Celebrity Fight Night, but he had his own list of demands, a group of three or four friends he wanted to bring to Arizona as his guests. He asked if we would accommodate their lodging needs and pick up their airline tickets. We respectfully declined.

I told Tom that, first and foremost, we were a charity event, and that our expenses were already exorbitant, given the quantity and quality of our celebrity guest list. I let him know that I was truly sorry, but we had to manage our costs wherever possible.

Yeah, I know. Duh.

Wrong answer.

If I had had a crystal ball, I would've said the following words instead:

"Tom, they're all our guests. Bring them all to our event. Bring your sisters, your brothers, your friends, your cousins, your dogs, your cats, whomever you desire."

I could never get him back after that.

2. Seating myself next to Blake Shelton, a country music star who is also a huge fan of the Arizona Cardinals. I later learned that Bruce Arians, former head coach of the Cardinals, was really upset and disappointed with me.

Arians was a marquee attraction in the NFL and immensely popular in Arizona. He expected to sit next to Blake, given their mutual interests and star power. I had forgotten they were good friends.

Anyone who has ever planned a wedding or bar mitzvah understands the perils of a seating chart, and how many egos are needlessly bruised when they're not sitting at a preferred table. It's a thankless job. But in retrospect, I should've had

Arians and Shelton sitting next to each other. Turnover on my part.

3. Not treating Céline Dion's husband like we treated Céline Dion. Celebrity Fight Night had lured one of the greatest female voices in the world to perform at our event when we successfully recruited Dion. In our excitement, I failed to seat Dion's husband and manager, René Angélil, next to our own guest of honor.

   Instead, I sat next to Muhammad Ali.

   Granted, I always wanted to sit next to The Champ, all the time, every day, no matter what event we were attending. I understood Ali and he understood me. But on that particular night, my wife got my attention. Nancy said, "Jimmy, you really need to let René sit by Muhammad."

   I moved out of the way and René relocated right next to Ali. And in the middle of her set, Céline stopped her performance and halted her band just to congratulate her husband on dining next to one of the most influential people in history. That's how much it meant to Dion and her husband. René had a huge grin on his face. I should've seen that coming.

4. Disturbing Garth Brooks. One of our more generous donors once pulled me aside during a Celebrity Fight Night and said he would make a nice gift to our foundation if I could somehow convince Garth Brooks to take the stage and perform one of his songs.

   By now, you know I love a good challenge. I know how to sell. I was suddenly looking at a potentially massive, unexpected donation to our foundation against the hassle of a five-minute vocal performance from one of my special invitees. How hard could that be?

I was determined to make it happen.

We pushed and prodded until Garth got up there against his wishes. I thought he was awesome.

Later, I found out Garth was not happy. He was not prepared to perform or be put on the spot like that. It was a mistake and I should've handled it differently. I was lost in a fundraising mindset and not the creative sensibilities of an artist I needed to protect. It was very disrespectful of me.

I sent a letter to Garth to apologize, and we buried the hatchet.

5. Pushing LeBron James. Twice, we auctioned off dinners with LeBron James that sold for over $100,000. One of the dinners was hosted at the Wynn Las Vegas hotel. The other was held in James's hometown of Akron, Ohio.

The second dinner was purchased by a father for his son, a kid who went to a private high school in Arizona. The father picked him up and they traveled to Akron. Can you imagine how excited that young boy must have been?

The dinner was scheduled for 6:30 p.m., and we got there in plenty of time. Everything was running like clockwork.

Then my phone rang. It was my cue that LeBron was arriving. I went outside to meet him and escort him inside the restaurant.

LeBron looked at me, and I could immediately tell something was wrong.

"Jimmy, I can't do this," LeBron says. "I don't feel good."

Oh no, I thought. "LeBron, you have to do this," I implored. "This gentleman we have seated inside was so generous and his son is so excited. He took him out of school just to come here. You've got to try to make this happen!"

Keep in mind, this was early in LeBron's career. I wouldn't have been talking to him like that if this was LeBron in his prime, or LeBron at the end of his career, as the reigning king of the NBA. So I pushed hard.

Finally, LeBron relented. He agreed to sit with us through dinner. He was all class, very attentive. I was extremely appreciative of his efforts.

Two days later, I read in the newspaper that LeBron had tested positive for Influenza A, better known as the swine flu.

I had to call the donor. I told him, "You know, you might want to see your doctor . . ."

6. Not listening to Kenny Rogers. During another Celebrity Fight Night, singer Kenny Rogers pulled me aside. He had been watching me facilitate meet and greets with Ali throughout the evening, and he thought I was pushing Ali too hard.

"Jimmy, he's a celebrity," Rogers said. "He wants his space. You're making it too hard on him."

Rogers didn't know and couldn't have known that Ali lived for human interaction, that he always wanted me to bring people in his direction. But in that moment, I realized how my actions regarding Ali might appear to others, the ones who didn't know him like I did.

7. Judging Steven Tyler. In Toronto, I attended David Foster's charity event, where Aerosmith singer and television star Steven Tyler was the headline performer. Foster asked me to do an invocation for about 1,500 people. I thought to myself, *Steven Tyler is probably the most disinterested person in this room when it comes to hearing me give an invocation.*

After the invocation, I received an incredible surprise. Steven was the first person to come up to me and compliment me on my choice in prayers.

So what I'm saying is, the prayer wasn't the mistake. It was the judging.

I thought, *Here's Steven Tyler with his long hair and his rock-and-roll attitude. He couldn't care less about a prayer.* That was stupid and wrong.

8. Being clueless with Dan Patrick. Patrick is a former ESPN personality and a media icon. He agreed to come to our fourth event several years ago at the Arizona Biltmore. And on the back nine of our golf outing, he told me he was excited to be emceeing the event later that evening.

    Then he asked if we had a teleprompter.

    I looked at Dan quizzically.

    "What's a teleprompter?" I asked.

    A disbelieving look spread over his face.

    Really. I had no clue.

    He explained to me the function of a teleprompter, and how a speech could appear in a rolling, scrolling format, allowing you to read typewritten words while looking directly into the camera.

    I told him we'd have one by the start of the event. And you know what? I made good on that promise.

9. Risking the safety of Kelly Clarkson and a room full of fans. One night, Kelly Clarkson was on stage and rolling hot, singing her heart out. She invited the crowd to join her on stage, overloading a temporary fixture in the ballroom of a luxury hotel.

    I'm an insurance guy. I know better.

Within sixty seconds, we had 300 people on stage. I look over and notice that my wife is dancing with Billy Crystal's wife. It was pure bedlam.

My managers told me the stage almost broke that evening. You could see it shimmering up and down, like a bridge during an earthquake, nearly buckling from the cumulative weigh. And if that stage had broken, there would've been sprained ankles, torn ligaments, and other assorted injuries.

We got away unscathed, but it was a big mistake. We should've had security in place safeguarding us from the hype and emotion of partygoers lost in the moment.

10. Overpromising and undelivering with Rod Stewart. As previously explained, it took a Herculean effort to land Rod Stewart. But when he showed up at Celebrity Fight Night, he hit me with an unexpected request. He wanted to go onstage earlier than scheduled. He wanted to perform at 9:00 p.m., earlier than most headliners at events like ours.

    I agreed. After all, it was my job to keep superstars happy at Celebrity Fight Night.

    In the process, I made the mistake of not seeing the big picture while trying to accommodate a music icon. I should have known that based on the event schedule, I would never be able to fulfill his request. He didn't get on stage until 10:15 p.m. He was very upset and even thought about leaving the event.

11. Also overpromising and undelivering with Jon Bon Jovi. There was miscommunication about when he would be performing, and Jon did not take it well. John Corbett was there and saw the whole thing. John is the actor from *My Big Fat Greek Wedding*, and he told me he had run into Bon Jovi in the restroom. He said Bon Jovi was fuming.

Good news is, the audience enjoyed Bon Jovi's performance. And I own the mistake for promising a superstar entertainer that he could perform earlier than previously arranged.

12. Once I introduced former heavyweight champion Ken Norton to actor/comedian Chevy Chase. Ken immediately spilled his glass of red wine all over Chase's sport jacket. Chevy might've been upset, but he certainly wasn't going to pick a fight with a legendary boxer.

13. The following anecdote didn't happen at Celebrity Fight Night. Far worse, it happened at a funeral. But this story must be told at some point:

I walked into the funeral. I was asked if I would say a few words about a friend of mine who had just passed away. I agreed.

I remember wishing they would've given me some time to prepare, to get the right words on paper, given the circumstances.

The funeral started with an opening prayer and a song. And then they called me up. With perfect poise, I began giving my somber remarks. I spoke in extremely general terms. I had the funeral program in my hand, but I hadn't looked at its content.

I paused for a moment to gather my thoughts. In the middle of the speech, I looked down at the program. I was horrified.

I realized I was eulogizing the wrong person! I was attending a funeral for a fringe friend whom I had mistaken for a different person entirely.

I was within twenty seconds of eternally embarrassing myself when I realized the magnitude of my error.

Ah, but a good point guard is always quick on his feet. I ad-libbed my way through my own horror, corrected my mistake in midstream, and no one ever knew the difference.

Until now.

CHAPTER 11

VIVA ITALIA!

Celebrity Fight Night Goes to Italy

THE COLOSSEUM IS THE MOST ICONIC SYMBOL IN ROME. IT has been declared one of the New Seven Wonders of the World, and it's by far the most visited landmark in Italy. It sits in the middle of a sprawling urban city, and as you stand before it, you can almost feel the weight of its dramatic, bloody history.

In 2017, it was the site of Celebrity Fight Night in Italy—and rare air for everyone involved.

Only a handful of entertainers have enjoyed the privilege of performing inside the Colosseum. They are the biggest names in the industry, like Paul McCartney, Elton John, and Ray Charles. Only a few could summon the necessary pull. Andrea Bocelli is one of them. He helped open the doors of the Colosseum to Celebrity Fight Night, and in doing so, he helped open the doors to an entire country.

Bocelli is a legendary tenor in Italy—his popularity second only to the Pope. His pandemic concert, Music for Hope, was streamed live from the Duomo di Milano on Easter Sunday 2020. It attracted the largest simultaneous audience for a classical live stream in YouTube history. He's that revered, and he's that popular.

Bocelli has helped make Celebrity Fight Night in Italy a coveted event that now features waiting lists, private planes, yachts, and some of the most unique experiences in entertainment history.

It was a remarkable, historic triumph when the Roman Colosseum embraced and hosted our event. The visuals were stunning. Elton John performed. Then Aerosmith's Steven Tyler. And, finally, Bocelli, of course, along with the omnipresent David Foster.

Elton John accepted our invitation without knowing where the event would be staged. Veronica Bocelli, who also serves as Vice Chairman of the Andrea Bocelli Foundation, later dropped a hint to Sir Elton, saying, "You know we'll be together on a special stage?"

When he learned he would be performing inside the Colosseum, he was floored.

Veronica later said it was like Elton John's reward for saying yes and agreeing to perform for charity.

There was another surprise for our guests. The gala dinner was held at a seventeenth-century gallery that is home to hundreds of artistic masterpieces. Everyone in attendance felt surrounded by greatness.

The following night, millions of Italians watched Bocelli's performance on television, but only 500 people were allowed inside the Colosseum. They were VIP clients from all over the world. The orchestra was comprised of young musicians from a well-known musical academy in Italy, all of them ranging from eleven to twenty years old. They brought a fresh energy that Bocelli loved. He said he chose an orchestra of kids because "kids are the future." It was quite a show.

There is a great video of the event on YouTube. There is a clip where you can even see Steven Tyler entering the Colosseum while chomping on a piece of gum. But here's what you don't see in the video: as Tyler took the stage to perform Aerosmith's smash hit "Dream On," he took the gum out of his mouth and stuck it underneath Elton John's piano. Elton would not have been pleased to see that.

At the end of the evening, Tyler and Bocelli closed the show by singing together to John Lennon's "Imagine." David Foster accompanied them on piano while sitting next to Sharon Stone. People were openly weeping.

Veronica Bocelli commented after the show that, in general, Americans are easily excited and prone to exaggerated reactions. She said we love to use words like "great" and "wow." She also noted that what we collectively experienced that evening truly left everyone speechless.

Over the course of its dark and ancient history, the Colosseum has featured dramatic, intense entertainment that Romans so dearly loved. The stadium has a history of violence and combat and fights that included both humans and animals. There was a time when the execution of prisoners happened daily at the Colosseum, featuring death by crucifixion. And people actually came to watch. The bodies were said to be taken out the west gate, which faced the setting sun.

They also say the best time to visit the Colosseum is at night when you can feel the wind and the darkness and all the ghosts. We were blessed with something that few artists ever experience, and I couldn't help but think the only thing missing was Muhammad Ali.

We were in an arena famous for staging fights, where there have been winners and losers. Ali was a real fighter. A real champion. He would have loved to have been in that arena with us, the headline attraction inside the Roman Colosseum. I wish he could have shared that experience.

Our Celebrity Fight Night events in Italy are celebrations of what make the country so great: music, art, culture, fashion, style, and food. The proceeds benefit the Andrea Bocelli Foundation's efforts to help children in Haiti, giving aid to schools, orphanages, and programs that provide much-needed assistance to impoverished communities.

We have engaged some of the most prominent Italian families, like the Ferragamo family who started with a cobbler who built a shoe empire; and the Cavalli family, a high-end Italian fashion house known for luxury clothing, perfumes, and leather accessories. Same with the Gucci family and the Armani family, who hosted private receptions at their stores in Florence and Rome. We also staged an event in Venice, a city built on water.

Other celebrities who have joined us in Italy include George Clooney, who proposed to his wife, Amal, at the Palazzo Vecchio during Celebrity Fight Night in Florence. That generated plenty of national publicity.

We've also been fortunate to have Nicolas Cage, Lionel Richie, John Legend, Sophia Loren, Brian McKnight, Smokey Robinson, Kix Brooks and Ronnie Dunn of Brooks & Dunn, Josh Groban, Kristin Chenoweth, Evander Holyfield, Melissa Peterman, Michael W. Smith, Bo Derek, and John Corbett attending.

Lionel Richie said of our Celebrity Fight Nights in Italy: "With everywhere I've been with Celebrity Fight Night, this is the best. Why? Because it's Italy!"

CHAPTER 12

BUILDING RELATIONSHIPS

From Big Events to the Little Things

*I*LIKE TO ENCOURAGE PEOPLE. I LIKE TO RECOGNIZE THEIR accomplishments. I like to celebrate their success by throwing parties and staging big events in their honor.

That's my idea of fun.

Once, I reached out to former Suns star Amar'e Stoudemire after he signed a $100 million contract to play for the Knicks.

"Have they officially welcomed you to New York?" I asked.

"No," he said.

"Well, let's do it!" I said. "We'll have it at The Plaza Hotel."

I put together an invite list. I contacted the Knicks and secured a ballroom at the Plaza. I knew this was a new beginning and a big step for Amar'e.

Eight years earlier, he had arrived in the NBA directly from high school, after a very rough upbringing. He took the league by storm and was an instant hit in Phoenix and a dominant NBA power forward.

But New York is a different animal. The pressures and media expectations are relentless and intense. It's not easy to be a star in the Big Apple. It's not for everybody. I felt it would be reassuring to Amar'e if he felt the strength and love of his friends just as he was embarking on a new chapter of his career.

Our impromptu welcoming party received a jolt of good fortune. I was staying next door at The Ritz-Carlton and just leaving for the event when I noticed Kareem Abdul-Jabbar in the lobby of my hotel.

I already knew Kareem. I insured him. I seized the moment.

"Kareem, we're about to do something very special for Amar'e," I said. "Why don't you join me? Why don't you come over with me and say a few words and welcome him to New York? It would mean a lot to Amar'e if you showed up."

"Let's go," Kareem said.

After Jerry Colangelo led Team USA to a gold medal performance at the 2008 Summer Olympics in Beijing, I noticed there was a significant lack of fanfare awaiting his return to the Valley.

This bothered me. Colangelo is one of the most influential men in Phoenix history. He helped build the city into what it has become today. His name is on the basketball court at the Naismith Memorial Basketball Hall of Fame. A statue of his likeness is on the campus of Grand Canyon University. But for all his great work, he never won an NBA title with his beloved Suns, a team he practically birthed in 1968.

In other words, the 2008 Olympics weren't just a smashing success. They represented his first real basketball championship.

I attended those Olympics in China. Colangelo allowed me to fly on the Team USA charter, along with Kobe Bryant, LeBron

James, Chris Paul, and the guys. The leadership Colangelo showed in restoring pride in our Olympic basketball movement was extraordinary. And I wanted to do something nice for him.

So we put together an event, giving the net proceeds to the Special Olympics. We had Doug Collins as our emcee, and that was special for a lot of reasons. Collins, who twice coached Michael Jordan, was a great speaker. He always wore his heart on his sleeve.

Collins was also an Olympic hero in 1972, part of a team that endured a gut-wrenching loss to the Soviet Union in Munich, Germany. Collins made two clutch free throws in the closing seconds of that game to give his team the lead after enduring a hard foul that left him woozy. What came next was one of the most controversial endings in the history of sports, and many believe the game was stolen from the Americans.

Collins and his teammates were so outraged they refused to accept the silver medals.

Fast forward to 2008: Immediately after winning the gold medal in Beijing, LeBron James and all his teammates sought out Collins at the broadcast booth. They dedicated their medals to him, paying homage to the Olympic championship he deserved to win thirty-six years earlier. Powerful stuff.

Even better, Collins's son, Chris, was an assistant coach on the 2008 Olympic team. That year, Colangelo made sure all the assistant coaches received gold medals of their own, because that's the kind of man he is. That allowed Chris to give his gold medal to his father, and justice was finally served.

In 1990, Nancy and I hosted a dinner party at our home for Arizona Senator Jon Kyl, who was seeking reelection. Our guest speaker was the forty-first president of the United States, George H.W. Bush. We quickly received a lesson in national security.

Secret Service descended upon my home. They searched every room of our house, including closets, rooftops, and under our bed.

These men surrounded our neighborhood prior to the president's arrival.

After spending several hours with President Bush, I felt we had become fast friends. His warmth, sincerity, and tremendous sense of humor made a very positive impression on my life. President Bush and I continued to correspond following the dinner at my home, and later, we received an invitation to join him and his family for lunch at their home in Kennebunkport, Maine.

It was an invitation my family could not refuse. My daughter, Jennifer, ended up playing tennis on the Bush family's private court against their local tennis pro. During lunch, President Bush and I talked about sports. The president mentioned a mixed doubles tournament scheduled for the Kennebunkport Tennis Club in six weeks. And that's when the president asked me a favor.

"Can you invite some celebrities to participate in this tournament?" the president asked.

I immediately thought of former Boston Celtics great Bob Cousy, with whom I often played during his visits to Phoenix. I invited Darryl Rogers, head coach of the Detroit Lions. They both accepted the invitation.

President Bush's team ended up facing Cousy's team in the finals of that mixed doubles tournament. There were at least 1,000 people in attendance. Cousy was hypercompetitive and wanted to win so badly on the president's home turf that he was diving to make shots on the tennis court.

Meanwhile, the crowd was definitely pro-Bush. It was fun to watch, and Cousy's team prevailed in the end, proving that great competitors always find a way to win.

Another time, I leaned on Dr. Jerry Buss to help reward my life insurance clients. By then, I knew if you wanted to find Buss, you had to get on plane to Las Vegas. He loved playing poker. He was also very generous.

Buss once mentioned that he was thinking about a fun invest-ment in Phoenix. He asked if I wanted in on the deal.

"Jimmy, the Phoenix Playboy Club is for sale," Buss said. "Let's buy it, you and I."

I told him my wife wouldn't like that idea very much. I also told him I was leading a Bible study. But I thanked him for the offer, and he completely understood my position.

Later I told Buss I wanted to collaborate on a special event. I wanted to buy every seat on an America West airplane and send my customers to a Lakers game. I told Jerry I would pay for everything if my clients could have dinner at the famed Forum Club and enjoy tickets to the game.

"Jimmy, this is one of the most creative ideas I've ever heard," Buss told me. "I'll tell you what I'll do. You bring them over on a plane. I'll have our bus pick you up on the runway of LAX. Come to my house. I'll put together a spread of appetizers and wine. They can tour the house. Then dinner at the Forum Club is on me."

Buss lived at a famous Hollywood address. He bought Pickfair, which was once the honeymoon house of actor Douglas Fairbanks and actress Mary Pickford.

In its heyday, Pickfair was considered second only to the White House in accommodating distinguished guests and many foreign dignitaries. The historical significance was not lost on my clients. Neither was the surprise appearance of The Gorilla, the famous Suns mascot who ran up and down the aisles of the airplane on our short flight home from Los Angeles.

When the Major League Baseball All-Star Game came to Phoenix in 2011, I decided it would be a great time to honor my good friend Reggie Jackson.

We brought in Muhammad Ali and Ernie Banks. We high-lighted Reggie's baseball career. Do you remember how he would nearly corkscrew himself into the ground when missing a pitch? I once told him I had as much fun watching him strikeout as I did watching him hit home runs.

Reggie was very polarizing. He was opinionated. Once, the Yankees were playing the Rangers and I was in Dallas. I attended a lunch with Reggie and famed broadcaster Howard Cosell. It was like, who is going to talk first? Where is this conversation going to go? I was a spectator. Reggie would kick me in my leg, underneath the table, whenever Cosell got on some kind of roll. It was a great lunch.

Reggie is also a tough guy and an intense competitor. He used to get all over guys who would show up out of shape to spring training. He thought that was an insult to professional athletics and the spirit of competition. He would tell them they should've stayed home, that they didn't deserve to be on a Major League Baseball field. That's just how he was. Put on the uniform and it was an ultimate competition to Reggie.

Some guys had a hard time with Reggie. One year, Reggie had thirty-seven home runs at the All-Star Break.

"How many guys in the dugout are truly happy for you when you hit a home run?" I asked him.

He could only name two teammates.

In the book of Corinthians, it says, "love is not jealous or boastful; it is not arrogant or rude" (13:4–5 RSV). You can't love people and be jealous of them at the same time. We're all human. We all feel insecurities because we're all imperfect. That's why it is important to try and lift people up, to put a smile on someone's face, to celebrate when they do something well and not just think of yourself.

Jackson was also the type who flourished in New York. And when it was his turn to speak at the luncheon, his opening statement was typical Reggie:

"First, I'd like to step out of character and show some humility by saying thank you."

Reggie was also captivated by the presence of Ali, as so many athletes were. And near the end of his speech, Reggie took a page out of Ali's playbook, playfully taunting The Champ in some good-natured smack talk, as if they were about to step into the ring.

So if you wanna say when, I might let it go ten
And if I'm feelin' fine, I'll let it go nine
And if it gets late, you might have to go in eight
And if he's thinking about Heaven, he's going in seven
And if he's looking for some kicks, he's got to go in six
And if he talks jive, he's going in five
And if he talks some more, I'm cutting it to four
And if he talks about me, he's going in three
And if that don't do, he's going in two
And if you want some fun, he's going in one
And if he don't want to fight, he can stay home that night!

The crowd loved it. So did The Champ.

When the Diamondbacks returned to Arizona for games six and seven of the 2001 World Series against the Yankees, there was a tremendous demand for tickets. The state of Arizona had never won a major professional championship, and, at the time, PGA star Phil Mickelson was one of my clients. He also had gone to college at Arizona State University, and he really wanted to be part of the experience.

I invited Mickelson and his agent, Steve Loy, to join me and my wife at the ballpark. We had four first-row seats, which were practically on top of Arizona's dugout. The Diamondbacks finally prevailed in game seven, staging a ninth-inning rally against one of the best relief pitchers in baseball history, Mariano Rivera. It was an incredible scene, and Mickelson told me repeatedly it was one of the biggest thrills he has ever experienced as a spectator.

If you know anything about Mickelson, you also know he is very generous. He knows how to show his gratitude.

The following day, I was in my office and my receptionist said Mickelson wanted to see me. I didn't have an appointment with him, so I really didn't know why he was in my lobby. I walked down the hallway to meet him.

With a big smile on his face, Mickelson said, "Jimmy, thanks for the great time I had as your guest at the World Series. I want you and Nancy to enjoy this matching set of golf clubs as a token of my appreciation."

Mickelson gave us both a new set of Callaway clubs along with a golf bag. I proudly accepted and gave him a big hug. It is no secret why Phil has so many fans on tour. I would like to add that Mickelson would be the first to give credit to his wife, Amy, for the success he has enjoyed as a professional golfer. Equally important, Mickelson is a tremendous father.

***

In 1983, leading up to Christmas, I remember having a conversation with my family focusing on how blessed we were to have so much. We decided we should do something for children who don't get bicycles or gifts for Christmas. We decided to host a bicycle party.

We recruited donors who sponsored bicycles. We purchased fifty of them and stashed them in our garage. Then we invited inner-city kids from poor families to our home. We brought in Suns announcer Al McCoy as our first emcee. Many of the kids were from broken homes and had no clue what was going on.

Until we rolled out the bicycles.

The excitement was palpable.

At one point, so many kids went into our house to use the bathroom that it overflowed, and water began streaming into the kitchen. My wife, Nancy, wanted to know what in the heck was going on.

"Sorry, honey. Next year will bring in a Port-a-John," I said.

She did not like the sound of that.

Our Bicycles for Kids program turned into an annual occurrence. During our first thirty-seven years, we've given away almost 10,000 bicycles.

Author Zig Ziglar and his wife, Jean, purchased bicycles for over twenty-five years before Zig's death in 2012. He always said, "Positive thinking won't let you do anything. But it will help you do everything better than negative thinking will."

While staging big events has become something of a passion, it's the little stuff that really matters.

I build business relationships by pursuing them and nourishing them. I work at it because I love it.

When I make a new business contact, I log important names and dates from that person's life into a calendar. They might be anniversaries, birthdays, or the names of children. But those dates become part my life. I try to always reach out on special occasions. It makes all the difference in the world.

I also believe in the three most important words in relationship building: keep in touch.

I wake up exceptionally early. I don't want to miss out on anything. I work silently and efficiently in the still of the night. Lionel Richie tells me he creates his best music in the middle of the night. I just seem to have great clarity at that time. I do my best work without interruptions.

I have spent hours reading headlines, learning pertinent developments that might affect friends all across the country, in different lines of work. I connect with them on matters of importance, and I always try to provide words of encouragement.

I have legal pads placed in strategic locations all over the place. I place them in my car, in my bathroom, and in my bedroom. I am constantly writing notes to myself. Too many good ideas float away forever if you don't write them down.

Networking is not a term I'm entirely comfortable with. Networking is often a selfish practice. It is built on keeping score and settling bets. It is quid pro quo. I will do this for you if you do this for me.

I don't like that approach. I believe in giving without asking whenever possible. I believe in offering my services without caveats and paybacks. I have seen firsthand the trust you can build when your motives are unselfish, especially with celebrity clients and friends. Trust is a powerful thing.

I am a hard worker, but I never want to be a workaholic. I never want to be someone who puts work ahead of family and spiritual life. That person's priorities are out of order. Someday, he or she will wake up older and wonder, *What happened to my life?*

Those people do not appear to understand their purpose in life.

Frankly, I want the rest of my life to be the best of my life. But I readily admit, it is easy for my plate to become overcrowded. I admit I have made the mistake of putting work ahead of family too many times. I don't think any businessman makes the claim that he spends too much time with his kids. Andrew Carnegie once said, "As I grow older, I pay less attention to what people say. I just watch what they do."

The world is also different now. In some ways, it's harder to meet people. The playing field has changed dramatically. Calling someone without texting for permission ahead of time is now considered an intrusion. Answering your phone is no longer an obligation or part of our social contract.

These days, actually talking to people seems to be the least appealing thing about a smartphone. Many people wear headsets and earphones in public as a way to put up "Do Not Disturb" signs. Sometimes we have so much tact, we have no contact.

We also live in a world that is angry, divided, and disconnected. It is more important than ever to nourish relationships and be a positive force in the world.

Keeping in touch requires discipline. It requires effort. When people don't hear from you, they forget about you.

Perhaps a businessman is struggling or being publicly criticized for a mistake. This is a time I like to reach out with encouraging words. I am constantly keeping in touch with our sports clients before and after their individual seasons have concluded. I am amazed at how often they need encouragement.

I have found some celebrities are the most insecure, shallow, and lonely people you will ever meet. I have also met fabulous celebrities who are just the opposite. There is something to be said about people who are not afraid to follow their dreams.

Do you remember Ivan Boesky?

He was involved in a Wall Street insider trader scandal in the mid-1980s. By 1986, he had amassed more than $200 million by betting on corporate takeovers. He was also featured on the cover of *Time* magazine.

By 1987, he was in prison, sentenced to three and a half years at Lompoc Federal Prison Camp in California. He was also fined $100 million.

I began reading numerous articles about Boesky. Recent stories indicated that he was seeking redemption and forgiveness. That caught my eye. C.S. Lewis once said, "Forgiveness sounds like a good idea until you have to forgive."

I decided to visit Boesky in prison. I contacted Lompoc to see how I could obtain permission. I wrote to Boesky several times and he wrote me back. In his letters, he expressed regret and disappointment. Eventually he invited me for a prison visit.

When I arrived for our sixty-minute window, I noticed Boesky had a remarkable tan and newly defined muscles. He told me spent most of his free time outdoors, lifting weights in the prison yard.

We talked about his feelings, his sorrow, and his sense of guilt. We prayed together, and he said he felt relief. I told him there would be consequences for his actions, that the outside world would treat him differently upon his release, and he would have to deal with a lot of negativity. I also told him to focus on his fresh start and the things that he could control. I have always felt you can't go back and change the beginning. But you can start where you are and change the ending.

He was released from prison the following year. We met at the Valencia Hotel in La Jolla, California, a year after that. And I haven't heard from him since.

Bruce McNall is a former sports executive who owned an NHL team (the Los Angeles Kings) and a Canadian Football team (the Toronto Argonauts). He's famous for bringing Wayne Gretzky to Southern California, for acquiring the greatest hockey player in the history of the sport. McNall's profile peaked in 1992 when he was elected chairman of the NHL Board of Governors, the second-highest post in the NHL.

I developed a relationship with McNall. I ran into him at Lakers games when we'd both be hanging out inside the Forum Club. Suddenly I began reading about his financial problems. Here's a guy who was once at the top of the world or not far from it. And in an instant, it seemed like he was stripped of everything. His world came crashing down.

I frequently corresponded with McNall while he was in prison, when he probably needed a few more friends. I have a feeling he appreciated those letters.

I try hard to not come across as overly aggressive when meeting people. I like to get acquainted in a casual and informal way, which hopefully comes across as natural. But you can't be shy even when there is the risk of rejection and a possibility of embarrassment.

There are times when I regret what I have said, when my approach was too bold. When maybe I interrupted people at the wrong time. That happens. Those are the inherent risks, and the rejections are nothing compared to the lifelong relationships I have built over the years.

You can't be afraid to take chances. I have never been hesitant to meet people or create a conversation, which is the lifeblood of building relationships. And, on occasion, I like to swing for the fences.

Shaquille O'Neal once called me "a low-level botheration." I think he meant I was a good friend and an occasional annoyance. I can live with that.

When Shaq became my client, we had to do a routine stress test on his heart. Dr. Richard Emerson was the Suns orthopedic surgeon and team physician at the time, and I put him charge of executing the physical.

I received a frantic phone call from Dr. Emerson where I could tell he was nervous.

"Jimmy, I'm really sorry," Dr. Emerson said. "But Shaq has been on this treadmill machine and he just broke it. A bunch of pieces fell off."

As you probably know, Shaq is extremely large. I have one of his shoes that he gave me as a souvenir. It's a size twenty-three and it looks like an aircraft carrier. And when Shaq started pounding up and down on this treadmill, it simply collapsed under his size and strength.

"Jimmy, I've never had this happen before!" Dr. Emerson said.

"Of course you haven't," I said. "You've never had someone as big as Shaq on your treadmill! But either fix the machine or get a new one because we have to get that test done today!"

Shaq is also extremely generous. He's proven that on many occasions. Once he even insisted on taking me shopping.

"Why?" I asked.

"Because you have helped me and my family with our retirement planning," he said.

I told him I didn't want him to buy me anything, that his friendship was more than enough.

"Jimmy, if you don't cooperate, I will put my bodyguard, Jerome, on you," he said.

I had no choice but to shut my mouth. I came home with a pair of beautiful Italian shoes for my wife.

There is a famous saying in the world of real estate. It is all about location, location, location.

In business and in life, I have learned it's all about relationships, relationships, relationships.

CHAPTER 13

UNIVERSITY OF ADVERSITY

Serving the Homeless at St. Vincent de Paul

*I*OWN A TUXEDO. I AM COMFORTABLE IN A BOW TIE. I KNOW HOW to smile for the cameras, including the ones I don't see. I'm a regular guy who learned how to move inside the celebrity fishbowl with my famous friends.

But some of my favorite and most important work is done behind the scenes, in much grittier conditions, in the dirt and shadows of downtown Phoenix. A place where there are no photographers and no red carpets. A place where not everyone smells so good.

I am extensively involved with the St. Vincent de Paul homeless shelter in Phoenix, where I am glad to donate my time and resources because the need is severe, the conditions are extreme, and because it is the right thing to do.

Show up any Monday at St. Vincent de Paul and you will likely see a line of 500–600 people winding out the front door and snaking down the block. That's because breakfast is being served—and so is hope.

Banners from our local sports teams hang from the ceiling, representing the Suns, Cardinals, Diamondbacks, Coyotes, Arizona State University, the University of Arizona, Northern Arizona University, and Grand Canyon University. The banners give people a sense of community, identification, and pride and remind them that they are part of a much larger family.

There are also sports uniforms hanging in the room: the No. 44 that Reggie Jackson wore for the Yankees; the No. 3 that Dwyane Wade wore for the Miami Heat; Larry Fitzgerald's No. 11; Anquan Boldin's No. 8; and even Meadowlark Lemon's Harlem Globetrotters jersey.

Reggie Jackson once said of St. Vincent de Paul, "I went to the homeless shelter Jimmy visits regularly and probably appreciated it more than he did because of what it did for me and the awareness it gave me as a person."

Actor Denzel Washington said, "The most selfish thing you can do is to help other people. Why do I say that? Because that's where gratitude comes in. That's where you get lifted up and you feel happiness in your life by helping other people."

Happiness can be thought, taught, and caught but never bought.

At St. Vincent de Paul, and any homeless shelter around the world, we are serving a segment of the population that is focused on bare essentials. These are people who are dealing with basic human survival, people who don't know where their next meal is coming from. It's humbling and it makes you appreciate the things we all take for granted.

I started our Never Give Up Program in 2008 at St. Vincent de Paul's shelter for the homeless. I open each meeting with short

messages of encouragement. Over the years, we have featured approx-
imately 400 guest speakers who also deliver inspirational speeches.
Those speakers have included businesspeople, doctors, attorneys,
housewives, and celebrities who have filled our calendar for more
than a decade. I am extremely happy with the quality of messages
and messengers we have brought to St. Vincent de Paul.

Plato once said, "Be kind, for everyone you meet is fighting a
hard battle." I believe we should all do a better job of encouraging
and seeing the best in others. Investment manager Foster Friess once
spoke at the shelter, and afterward, he hired about a dozen homeless men to clean up an area littered with glass and garbage. Friess
commented that many of the homeless have low self-esteem and
need encouragement.

In the movie *The Blind Side*, a wealthy family adopts a homeless
boy named Big Mike. During lunch at the country club, a friend tells
Sandra Bullock's character, "That's nice. You're changing that young
man's life." Sandra's character replied, "No, Big Mike has changed
my life." That's how I feel working with the homeless, which I've
been doing nearly every Monday morning since 2007, a streak that
was interrupted by the pandemic. Working with the homeless has
changed my life.

One morning, I picked up Andrea Bocelli at his hotel at 6:30
a.m. The night before he had performed at a concert, which meant
he didn't get much sleep. We arrived at St. Vincent de Paul thirty
minutes later. It was a chilly morning, probably forty degrees outside.
He sang "Ave Maria," which is Latin for "Hail Mary," a capella to
our morning crowd from the Meadowlark Lemon Basketball Court,
which was donated by Celebrity Fight Night. It was beautiful.

Every year at Vincent de Paul, we organize a steak dinner for
approximately 500 homeless people. I contact several of the top
chefs in Arizona, including Mark Tarbell, Chris Bianco, Marc
Lupino, and Vincent Guerithault. They love cooking for the

event, which we stage on January 17 in honor of Muhammad Ali's birthday. It is always choice steak, but we have to make sure it's cut up in little pieces, because many of the homeless are missing teeth.

We also have an annual pizza and ice cream party on June 3 in memory of Ali's death. Most everyone we serve remembers The Champ, who absolutely loved to spend time with the people at St. Vincent de Paul.

This is how Steve Zabilski, executive director of St. Vincent de Paul, recalls our modest beginnings:

> Jimmy started a Bible study at St. Vincent de Paul for the homeless. At the very beginning there were four to five people and a couple of them were sleeping. I kid Jimmy that those who weren't sleeping were there for the coffee. But until COVID-19 changed our operations, Jimmy showed up every Monday morning at 7:00 a.m. for twelve consecutive years to fuel the Never Give Up program he started for the homeless.
>
> Most people think of St. Vincent de Paul as a place that provides food and shelter, which we do. But Never Give Up is something that gives people hope. It gives them a chance to reflect on the challenges they've had. They hear a diverse lineup of people and celebrities standing before them and personalizing their own troubles. It gives them a sense of hope, a feeling that they're not alone.
>
> What Jimmy has done here has taken St. Vincent de Paul to a whole new level. We like to say that this not just a soup kitchen.

Frankly, I have two heroes in Phoenix at St. Vincent de Paul: Steve Zabilski, the executive director at SVdP, and Jerry Castro, who is the general manager at SVdP. Both have committed their lives to helping the homeless.

I didn't plan on this journey. I became involved with St. Vincent de Paul in 2001 after my daughter Jennifer asked me to volunteer. She worked full-time at the charity, and I politely declined.

I didn't want to get my hands messy. I told her I was too busy.

I immediately felt an acute sense of shame. Why was I so reluctant to serve the weak and less fortunate as God commands? What did that say about me? I was making excuses, convincing myself that I was too busy.

I was putting my own needs first, rationalizing everything and anything. I told myself that I couldn't singlehandedly make a difference in the lives of Arizona's homeless population, and I believed that whatever money I donated would be wastefully spent. And, really, I didn't have the time.

The list of excuses went on and on. It's called my Cop-out List.

I finally decided to visit, and it was a life-changing event for me.

When I first volunteered in 2001, I met a man who was very dirty and disheveled. He reached out to shake my hand, but I was very slow to react.

He saw right through me.

"You don't want to shake my hand, do you?" he said.

"Yes, I do," I lied.

"No, you don't," he said.

He walked away with a sad, disgusted look on his face.

I felt awful. At that moment, I had an epiphany. My heart was dirtier than his hand. Jimmy Walker needed to change.

At St. Vincent de Paul, I felt a different kind of reward. I received no pay or credit, but my work was directly benefitting those who needed it the most. These people made me better. They inspired me to make them better. It became one of my life's true passions to deliver the most relevant guest speakers to St. Vincent de Paul. Most of the names you have read about in this book have answered the call to speak at St. Vincent de Paul, and I love them for their generosity.

Once the keynote speaker has finished, I always share a parting message with the crowd, highlighting a couple of positive things our guest speaker may have shared.

I let them know how St. Vincent de Paul can help improve their lives, whether they are battling addictions or other self-destructive tendencies. I remind them that they can attend meetings that are available every day for anyone struggling with their addictions. Ultimately I just want them to know that people care. They need to know they are not worthless outcasts. They need to know they are important enough to matter. The most important message I give them is: "God loves you and knows your potential."

I have heard their stories. I met a forty-year-old homeless man whose only possession was a blanket. I couldn't figure out why he was struggling so badly. He was a good-looking guy. He was a graduate of the University of Oklahoma, a former player under head coach Barry Switzer. He was also homeless because of his alcoholism.

Former Notre Dame head football coach Lou Holtz is a close friend of mine, and he once said, "I've never met a man who is at peace with a job who said, 'I owe all my success to drugs and alcohol.'"

When I arrive on the campus of St. Vincent de Paul, I feel like I am arriving at the University of Adversity. You meet people who are hurting tremendously, on the inside and the outside. People who were knocked down by one obstacle too many, by that one bad break crippling their spirit.

I encourage them to simplify. To forget the cruelty and injustice of what they've experienced. To find something positive in their lives and build upon that. To not compare themselves with others. I remind them we all have problems and it is important not to blame others for the difficulties they might be facing.

Sympathy is important. But so are expectations. It's important for everyone to set goals. That includes homeless people.

I remind them of something *New York Times* bestselling author Harvey Mackay once told me: The biggest room in the world is the room for improvement.

Craig Weatherup, retired CEO of Pepsi, who is highly successful and respected in the corporate world, repeatedly shared with the homeless during his message that they would make it by not giving up.

During one of our meetings at St. Vincent de Paul, a homeless woman kept asking my name. She kept asking me how to spell my surname. I had no idea what was happening until the end of the meeting, when she handed me a check for $10.

She had spelled my name perfectly. I was moved to tears. A woman who possessed very little wanted to give back very badly.

I gave her a big hug. I was in awe of her generosity and humility. I accepted the check even though I knew she couldn't afford to make any kind of donations.

I later understood that she gave because she couldn't afford not to—because giving that check wasn't a random gesture. It was something that strengthened her own faith. It kept her world moving forward through all the turmoil.

I wasn't sure what to do with that $10 check. A few hours later, a ten-year-old boy walked through my office raising money for Muscular Dystrophy. At that moment, I knew exactly what to do with her contribution.

One Monday morning, a man stood up in our meeting and told the crowd he needed to quit blaming others for his problems. Everyone applauded.

Working with the homeless puts everything in perspective. Following the lead of Walmart founder Sam Walton, I always make sure my first meeting of the week is the best meeting of the week.

For me, that's a 7:00 a.m. pep rally at St. Vincent de Paul every Monday morning where I try to motivate and inspire. Even I often borrow the words of others.

One of Winston Churchill's most famous speeches consists of only ten words. He said, "Never give up. Never give up. Never, never give up."

I like to remind myself of another phrase when things seem to be going well: "Be humble or you'll stumble."

Oprah Winfrey had a better saying: "Be thankful for what you have; you will end up having more. If you concentrate on what you do not have, you will never, ever have enough."

Melani Walton, wife of Rob Walton, the chairman of Walmart, both attended our Never Give Up program at St. Vincent de Paul and encouraged the homeless to make good choices. At one time, Melani was a star basketball player. She spoke about the importance of doing your best to find a job even though you are facing many difficult challenges.

Every year in the months of May and June, I challenge the men and women at St. Vincent de Paul. I target Mother's Day and Father's Day, respectively. I know many of the folks we serve at St. Vincent de Paul haven't talked to their parents in years. It's heartbreaking that a large number of them are carrying grudges against their parents, and I have discovered that many of them carry anger towards their dads for abandoning them and leaving home.

I encourage them to let down their guard. I tell them to let go of their negative baggage and to call their parents—even offering for them to use one of our phones at St. Vincent de Paul, free of charge.

Once I met a homeless man named Frank who was estranged from his biological father. Frank told me his father was a philanderer, that he ran around with other women, that he had a drinking problem, and that eventually he left his mother. Frank told me he never really knew his father.

"Can you forgive him?" I asked Frank.

I challenged him to call his father.

He looked at me like I was crazy.

I stood my ground. And that year, Frank called his dad, wishing him a happy Father's Day.

Frank said his dad was dumbfounded. He apologized for not being a good father, for not being there when it mattered. Powerful stuff. I really believe the number one problem in America today is dysfunctional families.

During the 2009 NBA All-Star Game festivities, Dwyane Wade and his mother, Jolinda, spoke before a gathering at St. Vincent de Paul. Wade's mother shared with our audience how she wasn't always the famous mother of an NBA star, how she was once homeless and addicted to drugs.

She never gave up. She found strength in her darkest times. And later in life, Dwyane Wade purchased a church for his mother on the South Side of Chicago, where Jolinda Wade assumed the role of pastor. After her speech, I flew to Chicago to have lunch with Jolinda because I wanted to see her church.

"I don't think I've ever went through anything harder in sports than she went through in her life…with drugs, with jail, without her family," Dwyane said.

🏀 🏀 🏀 🏀 🏀

A homeless man once confronted me as I walked into St Vincent de Paul.

"What are you doing here?" he challenged me. "Are you homeless? What do you know about being homeless? Are these celebrity speakers you bring here homeless?"

"No, they are not homeless," I replied. "But many of them have problems just like you and me."

Another homeless man said to me, "I shouldn't even be in this room. I have held a gun to another man's head. I have broken into buildings and stolen things. I don't even deserve to be here."

I shook his hand. I told him that none of us were worthy of being in that room, that we have all relied on God's grace and forgiveness.

One day, two brothers were reunited in the dining room of St. Vincent de Paul. They were both in their fifties. Each carried a blanket and a knapsack. They hadn't seen each other for twenty-five years. Their paths randomly crossed in our shelter.

Can you believe that?

Once I met a man in his forties. He told me he was diagnosed with terminal cancer at age sixteen and that he had three months to live. He said his parents had even picked out a casket.

Well, not so fast. He had beat that diagnosis by twenty-four years. He showed me a tattoo on his chest that read, "Never Give Up."

I liked that a lot.

We often come to our Never Give Up meetings bearing gifts. We generally have twenty sponsored drawings where we give away $10 McDonald's gift cards. The joy among recipients is almost unbearable.

One man said the gift card would provide one ninety-nine-cent hamburger for each of the next ten days. I admired his long-term planning.

Another winner said he was heading over to McDonald's to get a hot fudge sundae at that very moment.

"At 8:15 in the morning?" I said.

His smile assured me there was no questioning his decision.

A seventy-five-year-old homeless man won a $10 gift card and began to bawl. He said he had never won anything in his life.

A young mother won a $10 gift card and also began to weep.

"I'm so happy!" she said. "Now I can give my daughter a birthday present!"

Once we brought in former Suns All-Star Cedric Ceballos to speak at St. Vincent de Paul. When the speech was over, I was approached by the tallest homeless man I had ever seen in my life.

He was nearly six foot ten. He wanted to speak with Ceballos. He also said he wanted to try out for the Suns.

He was forty-five years old and barely 145 pounds.

Cedric spent time with the homeless man. He couldn't get him a job on the Suns, but in the following week, Ceballos made sure he dropped off some of his old clothes for the man, which fit almost perfectly.

Where else was a six-foot-ten homeless man going to find secondhand gear from a six-foot-seven NBA star?

I have learned that being financially successful is not the ultimate victory in life. It's not always about money. It's about the journey and the lives we can touch, the legacy we can leave, and the world we can change for the better. I have a hard time driving by a homeless person on the street without stopping and offering my help. I usually ask two questions: Are you homeless? What's your name? The last part is really important because homeless people love to hear their names because they are rarely addressed by their names.

Usually I'll give that person a $5 gift card to McDonald's along with a parting message: "God loves you. Never give up." I usually get a smile in return.

Over the course of my life, I have attempted to parlay my good fortune and goldmine of relationships into the collective good of the community. I've rarely had an athlete, entertainer, or celebrity turn down a chance to speak to the homeless at St. Vincent de Paul. That says so much about the goodness inside all of us.

Also, I've rarely had a speaker who wasn't deeply moved by the experience.

NFL star Larry Fitzgerald is considered royalty in Arizona, and he delivered a heartfelt message to awestruck attendees. He encouraged the audience to work hard, keep a good attitude, and never give up. A few weeks earlier, Pro Bowl wide receiver Anquan Boldin brought his Bible and read the story from the book of Joshua, how Joshua led the Israelites to the Promised Land.

"God never fails," Anquan said.

Nancy Lieberman, a Hall of Fame women's basketball player, said this of her experience at St. Vincent de Paul:

> So many of us are blessed in our lives to do something that we love. Sometimes, you are around people who are less fortunate. I really do think sometimes there is a propensity to look down on people instead of reaching out to people. I don't know if [the intimacy] scares us, but people need us.
>
> I was never homeless, but I was a poor kid growing up in New York City. I know what it's like to have the lights turned out in my house. I know what it's like not to have heat or air conditioning. But we all have a heart and we all have the ability to give.

I've seen small miracles happen at St. Vincent de Paul. Maybe I've played a small role in helping some of those miracles happen. I know this for a fact: People who volunteer at St. Vincent de Paul carry their experiences back into their own worlds, back to their families, their friends, and their co-workers. It's a powerful, wonderful force to unleash on the world.

Servant leaders set powerful examples. They defy traditional leadership models because they put people ahead of power. More than 200 scriptures in the Bible deal with helping the poor. I believe God is trying to get our attention. One of my favorite scripture passages in the book of James urges us to not show favoritism to the rich or look down upon the poor (2:1 TLB). Don't be afraid to put the interests of others ahead of your own.

Serving others makes the world a better place. Serving others makes us better spouses, better friends, better parents, better role models, better business leaders, and better humans.

Warren Buffett said, "You should be doing things that change lots of lives."

Working with the homeless puts it all into perspective for me. Like Samuel Johnson said, "The true measure of a man is how he treats someone who can do him absolutely no good."

Too often we are driven by greed and selfishness. It's an easy trap entangling our best intentions. But when we serve, we give a gift that cannot be measured by human standards.

Ralph Waldo Emerson said, "The purpose of life is not to be happy. It is to be useful, to be honorable, to be compassionate, to have it make some difference that you have lived and lived well."

We all win when putting others first.

CHAPTER 14

LOSING OUR SON

In Memory of Scott Walker

THERE IS NO GREATER PAIN AND LOSS IN LIFE FOR A PARENT than losing a child.

That's why December 12, 2019, remains the worst day of my life. It was the day I learned my forty-three-year-old son, Scott, died from an accidental overdose.

The pain was so strong I thought my heart was going to jump out of my chest. It was heartbreaking and very sad. I did not want to believe this terrible news. I quickly realized how much I loved Scott and how much I would miss him.

I'm sure any parent would run into a burning building to save their child because the love for our children is greater than our fear.

Recently, I heard Andrea Bocelli singing, "Time to Say Goodbye." I broke down on the spot. Tears were streaming down my face because I did not have a chance to say goodbye to my son.

As a family, we find joy in knowing Scott is at home with the Lord and that he is no longer suffering from his disease. But his gain is our loss because he is greatly missed.

Since Scott's passing, I have had a wake-up call about life.

I am not the same person. I find myself praying more often, hugging and appreciating my wife more often, reading the Bible more often. My advice to parents is to hug your kids every chance you get. Tell them you love them every chance you get. You don't know when it's going to be the last time. We should not take our relationships with our children for granted.

I talk to Scott every day, and I thank Scott for helping me grow a deeper relationship with God.

Our close friend Nancy Hanley said to me, "I bet you want to use Scott's passing to help other people."

She was correct.

In memory of Scott, we decided to create our first nonprofit, Christian-based sober living home in Phoenix. My wife, Nancy, and my two daughters, Laurie and Jennifer, all played key roles. In addition, our current board members have been a huge help. Those include Grant Sardachuk, Mark Buckley, Rod Bentley, John Langbein, Andre Wadsworth, and our advisor Jennifer Evans.

Grief produces strong emotions. I believe some people never deal directly with the grief in their life. They stuff it down and pretend it doesn't exist. That's why they are still struggling with the emotional pain from the loss of a loved one, even if the traumatic event happened many years earlier.

Scott was not a quitter. He went to detox twenty-seven times to defeat his addiction. He went to three different thirty-day rehabilitation programs. Each time he was discharged, we felt the hope that he could remain sober.

He met regularly with his sponsor, Rod Bentley, who had been sober for many years. They would consistently go through the

Alcoholics Anonymous twelve-step program. Scott received much support from his friend, John Langbein, his financial advisor, Grant Sardachuk, Todd Borowsky, and Pat Manley.

Bentley truly comforted our family when he told me the following:

> Scott had a big heart and loved both you and Nancy deeply. You were amazing parents. I know. He would tell me about his good upbringing. I know. You helped his loving heart grow. I know. He would share from the bottom of his heart that your family meant the world to him. He admired you, your strength and faith. He never meant to hurt any of you. He loved you. I am a better man knowing Scott and your family. A true privilege.

Oswald Chambers said, "When you go through the loss of a loved one, the things we are going through are either making us sweeter or better men and women, or they are making us more critical and fault-finding."

My last visit with Scott came a few days before his death.

"Dad, the sober living home I am staying in is not being run correctly," he told me. "It's owned by businessmen and all they want to do is make a profit. I want to start a Christian-based sober living home to help people with the same disease that I have."

I made Scott a promise on the spot.

"Scott, I will help you build that sober living home," I said.

Three days later, our family received word that Scott had passed. The memories of losing Scott flood my mind every day.

I have never dealt with greater pain and hurt. The right song at the wrong time can bring heavy tears rolling down my cheeks. Since Scott's passing, there are still some nights where my pillow is wet with tears.

There is a myth that says God wants you to walk around with a smile on your face all the time, saying, "Praise the Lord." That is not how it works. We won't always have smiles on our faces because life can be very difficult. The greatest king of Israel was David, and he cried out to the Lord and said, "God, I'm hurting. I'm grieving." David spilled his guts and told God he was living in a difficult time.

I would like to encourage people like our family who are dealing with grief to trust God, who can begin to help heal your heart.

Scott's legacy can be viewed in four different parts.

1. Scott loved the Lord and his family very much. He also enjoyed business, hunting, and fishing.
2. Scott was very smart and must have had a very high IQ. Plus, he had an excellent sense of humor.
3. Scott would give the shirt off his back to help anyone in need.
4. Scott enjoyed following sports teams. And when he was younger, he played in national tennis tournaments, where he was very competitive.

Jerry and Joan Colangelo are among our closest family friends. Jerry said of Scott:

> Scott was a very bright young man and it was obvious he would be very successful in whatever field he chose. Scott chose insurance and he became very successful in the industry. I choose to remember Scott as this bright, intelligent, and effervescent young man who had many dreams. His life ended way too short. Yet I know that because of his faith, which was very, very strong, that he is in Heaven with his Lord and Savior, Jesus Christ. And that he will be reunited with his family in the future.

Scott loved and had the best mom in the world. During Scott's last two years, he would talk to his mother almost every night. Sometimes their visit would last for over an hour. Scott would do 95 percent of the talking while Nancy would listen patiently, offering some words of wisdom and encouragement. Many times, their conversations would end with a prayer.

Following high school, Scott attended Colorado State University and started marketing life insurance after college. Scott was very well educated. He was a licensed CLU (Chartered Life Underwriter) and ChFC (Chartered Financial Consultant), plus he had his securities licenses to market Variable Life insurance policies. Scott easily passed those tests since he was very smart and was a quick learner. Personally, I would need five times as much studying to pass those same tests.

Scott was also a good teacher with the insurance agents who worked with him. David Mathias, one agent, said, "I would not be the person I am today in business or life if it weren't for my six years that I spent working with Scott."

During the last three years of Scott's life, he was not in denial about his disease. He was very open about his illness. He recruited many of his friends to attend Alcoholics Anonymous meetings when he recognized others with addiction issues. One of his clients was former NFL star Andre Wadsworth, who started Impact Church in Scottsdale, where Scott regularly attended, inviting many of his friends to join.

Wadsworth said:

Genuine, loyal, dependable, and loving are the words to describe Scott Walker. *Genuine* because when I first connected with Scott, it was for business purposes. But thirty minutes into the meeting, we started talking about life. I am not sure why but we both opened up about real things like struggles, failures, and successes. It is very seldom you meet someone for the first time who lets down their guard and you reciprocate the same, but I realized later that is who Scott was.

I know from the first day we connected Scott would be a friend and he would be loyal, even to his own hurt. Being a former athlete, loyalty resonates with me, so I recognized that character trait in him pretty quickly. I got to see from Scott that when he talked about his family, obviously it was unfiltered and raw. Scott left an impression on my life, and because of him, I live my life more vulnerable than ever!

One of Scott's clients was Craig Weatherup, the former CEO of Pepsi.

"Scott was invaluable to me," Weatherup said. "I had a very complicated situation involving a very old but very large split-dollar policy. And Scott led the effort to coordinate a unique restricting that left everyone satisfied. I will forever be grateful for Scott's creative brilliance."

Scott developed an outstanding national reputation for being one of the finest financial strategists in the country.

I have been marketing life insurance since high school, and I have never met anyone in our business that had better marketing skills and cared more about their clients than Scott.

I make it a habit of carrying a small, wooden cross with me every day, a reminder to be thankful for my blessings, a reminder of the ultimate sacrifice ever made. Occasionally, Scott would ask if I had any additional crosses to give away to certain friends. He had a personal relationship with the Lord. He often came to me and would say, "Dad, let's pray."

When Scott was younger, we attended basketball games at the Forum in Los Angeles, where we would have dinner with Lakers owner Dr. Jerry Buss in the famed Forum Club.

Once Nancy and I were guests of Buss at the horse races in Del Mar. Scott was around ten years old at the time, and I gave him $5 to bet on each race. My son also noticed how intensely Buss studied the horses and the jockeys. He could tell Buss was very knowledgeable when it came to handicapping a race. So my son made his bets by looking over Buss's shoulder and betting on the same horse. Scott went home with $300 that afternoon.

Like I said, my son was very smart, even at a young age.

Sean Currie, executive director of Celebrity Adventures, said, "Scott many times contacted me with some good ideas regarding which celebrities he would like for us to invite to our event."

Scott would tell me many times over the years, "Dad, I would take a bullet for you." I always thought that comment was very unusual to repeatedly make over the years, but I knew Scott was trying to tell me how much he loved me, and that no matter the circumstances, he wanted to protect me.

After Scott's passing, our pastor at Scottsdale Bible church, Jamie Rasmussen, counseled Nancy and I by sharing scriptures that gave us much comfort in our grieving.

Well-known pastor and author of *The Purpose Driven Life* Rick Warren came to Phoenix and gave us counsel. He said grieving is important, and that everybody grieves differently. I continue to grieve every day and will until I hug Scott in Heaven.

Grief reminds me that life on Earth is a struggle. I am also learning that God can do something good in our lives during painful times. God can use our grief to get our attention and renew our focus. God has used my grief to build my trust in Him. I know He can bring good out of bad. My hope is in God, and I know He is not going to waste an ounce of my pain.

I don't think we grieve very well. We don't see it as a good thing. But it is. Grief is the price tag of losing someone we love very much. If we never grieve, it means we're out of touch with reality. Grief is painful, but it is also healthy. For many people, though, the grief is so painful that they don't want to walk through it. So they get stuck emotionally. We should see grief as a gift from God because it helps us get through the tough seasons of life. Pastor Warren told us that when you experience a painful loss like we did in losing a child, you need to grieve over it.

In our grief, we often are left with more questions than answers. Why do bad things happen? I don't know. Why did Scott die? I don't know. But I do know that God has the answers. I know He loved Scott and our family, and I know He has a plan whether it makes sense to me or not. Rather than asking why, I'm asking what.

What can I learn from this? What can I do for God's glory and to help others? I believe when we put our trust in God, our greatest ministry comes out of our struggles and weaknesses.

Scott's death will never make sense to me, and the pain of losing him will never go away. But in the midst of it all, I truly believe that hope is available to all of us, where we can experience joy and peace today knowing the certainty of Heaven that awaits us.

God's strength is always sufficient.

Circumstances may appear to wreck our lives. However, God can use them to rebuild our lives.

I knew our only option was to trust God and let Him lead us through the pain. Even though we didn't understand why this had happened, our job was to persevere and continue to follow the Lord.

When Scott was twelve years old, he accepted Christ. Scott attended some Christian camps like Kanakuk in Branson, Missouri, and Young Life camps in Colorado. He was never ashamed of his faith in Jesus.

I was standing over Scott's casket and preparing for the visitation when it finally began to sink in. It finally became real. I was never going to see him again. Life will never be the same again. Scott was kind, smart, gentle, loyal, sensitive, and handsome. So many people who loved Scott attended his service.

We were determined to make Scott's funeral a celebration of his life. We called it a "homecoming." We took comfort in knowing he is now in Heaven. The service was a blessing for us, and from the comments I heard afterward, I believe it was a blessing for others as well. I spoke for about ten minutes, not knowing if I would be able to get through my speech without breaking down. With the Lord's strength and wisdom, I talked about Scott's life on Earth, and more important, his eternal life through Jesus.

We don't know much about Heaven—and we won't until we arrive. I do know that I will not be completely healed until I meet Scott there. I also know that if my son called me from Heaven, he would probably say to me, "Dad, you are so wrong! Heaven is much cooler than you ever said!"

Scott was very close to his older sisters, Laurie and Jennifer. He would do anything for them. Scott was very proud of them for their excellent family values. He also had good relationships with his brothers-in-law, Ethan Frey and Jon Hunter. He loved going to the hoop on the basketball court with his nephews. He loved to spend time with our grandchildren.

Our first Grace Sober Living Home opened in the summer of 2021, housing seven men who are recovering from their addiction. We plan to open more Sober Living Homes in Phoenix and Scottsdale, of which Scott would give full approval.

The majority of sober living homes have become lucrative businesses. Ours is nonprofit. The home is an alcohol- and drug-free environment for individuals recovering from their addictions and their disease. These residences are less restrictive than treatment programs. Residents can attend school, go to work, and enjoy social functions while living in our home. But we require participation in twelve-step meetings, ongoing counseling, and a contribution to making their environment clean and inviting for everyone. In addition to periodic Bible study, our Grace Sober Living Homes will have a basketball hoop, a ping pong table, weights, exercise equipment, and other activities to help residents through their recovery process.

Our mission is to decrease the relapse rate of addiction and help people reach optimal wellness. Scott would want us to help others find the right path.

We have called our first sober living home Scott's Place.

CHAPTER 15

THE WAR ON DRUGS

A Country in Crisis

*A*DANGEROUS WAVE OF DRUG ABUSE IS SWEEPING ACROSS America. Deaths from overdose have reached an all-time high.

In the past three decades, drug overdoses have killed approximately 870,000 people.[1] Drug abuse is responsible for more deaths than any other health condition, and the problem has reached a breaking point.[2]

The Centers for Disease Control and Prevention reported 93,331 fatal overdoses in 2020, a 29 percent increase over the previous year.[3] *Twenty-nine percent.* It marks a record high for deaths from overdose, and most of the drugs entering our country are from Mexico and China.

The numbers paint a clear picture of our Opioid crisis, which began in the 1990s with overdose deaths from prescription opioids. The second wave began in 2010 with a spike in deaths involving heroin, an unintended consequence to a medical industry that began to closely monitor and limit the abundance of opioid prescriptions, forcing addicts to seek a new supply chain.

The third wave began a few years later, with a considerable spike in overdose deaths involving fentanyl.

Fentanyl is a synthetic opioid. It is not derived from a plant, namely the opium poppy. It has a potency significantly higher than heroin. It is spreading rapidly across the country and expanding into other drug supplies. Many overdose deaths involving cocaine and counterfeit pills now involve fentanyl.[4]

Finally, the pandemic put our drug crisis over the top. It created additional stress in our daily lives. It created social isolation. It created a new set of mental health issues, where depression and loneliness were through the roof.

The pandemic caused a lot of people to use drugs more frequently and more recklessly. It forced many addicts to use alone, creating vulnerability. It disrupted their normal method of drug acquisition, creating volatility. Plus the economic stress of a pandemic played a significant role, creating a new wave of addicts.[5]

Many people were evicted during the pandemic. The crisis of homelessness was an epidemic in the country long before COVID-19, and studies show those who become dislodged, unmoored, or unhoused are much more receptive and irrational in their approach to drugs.

Just say no?

Solutions are far more complex than they sound.

Let's not be hypocrites. America has long been fueled by drug use, legal and otherwise. There are drugs to speed you up, slow you down, and put you to sleep. Nicotine. Caffeine. Viagra. Ambien. Adderall. Steroids. Human Growth Hormone. Opioids. They're all part of our tapestry, a country always on the lookout for some miracle pill or performance-enhancing agent to propel them through life's daily struggles.

But this is different.

Before synthetic drugs, a previous generation could feel fairly confident in drugs purchased on the street. Not anymore.

So here is my appeal to young people who have resisted the allure and forces of peer pressure when it comes to drug use:

There is not a community in America safe from synthetic opioids. Fentanyl is like a wildfire burning out of control. You do not know what you are buying, what you are taking, or what you are risking. Fentanyl does not discriminate. It kills the rich and famous, like Prince and many others. It kills teenagers looking for a good time. The potential reward is not worth the worst-case scenario, which happens far more often than you might think.

To those who wrestle with addiction, and to those who may not remember a life before drugs:

People struggling with opioid addiction need a lot of assistance to get their lives back on track. Please get the help you need and deserve before it is too late.

The National Institutes of Health surveyed more than 3,600 people between the ages of thirteen and twenty-two who survived an opioid overdose. Only one-third received any kind of follow-up treatment. Less than 2 percent received comprehensive treatment, including medication and behavioral interventions. Many pediatricians and family doctors are slow to recognize the symptoms of opioid addiction or advise proper courses of treatment.[6]

But those who survive an opioid overdose dramatically increase their chances of dying from a second overdose.[7]

Opioid addiction rewires the brain. Willpower is not enough find a way out or sustain recovery.[8] Immediate, effective treatment is critical.

Please take it from me: I am a grieving parent who has lost a son to drug abuse.

Drug abuse starts off as a dirty secret. It requires disabling critical thinking. It forces a person to devalue their life, their gifts, and their God-given blessings. It drives a wedge between users and people who love them most, because those loved ones are now considered dangerous because they can easily spot marked changes in a user's behavior. It's heartbreaking.

In the throes of addiction, nothing matters but the next score, the next hit, and the next high. Drugs diminish your identity and dissolve your standards. They will kill your soul. They will become your master. Drugs will not inform you of your condition until it's too late.

Give yourself a real shot at redemption. Give the people who love you one last chance, or you will burden them with hellish guilt and an unbearable sense of grief. Because no one helped. Because no one could get through. Because death by overdose means one day too late.

Throughout the years, I have had the opportunity to reach out to several troubled NBA stars. I have always believed that difficult times offer an excellent opportunity for personal growth. Granted, it was a different era.

Start with the scandal that rocked the NBA and the city of Phoenix.

Walter Davis was a highly decorated performer. He starred at the University of North Carolina and won an Olympic gold medal in 1976. He was Michael Jordan's favorite player growing up. He was drafted by the Phoenix Suns and became an instant fan favorite, inspiring many nicknames like "The Greyhound," "Sweet D," The Candy Man," and "The Man with the Velvet Touch."

He was also involved in a cocaine scandal that implicated Davis and five other current or former members of the Suns. The news was stunning. Davis had been a great ambassador for the franchise.

He was viewed as role model, and one of the classiest players in the NBA. He was a prolific scorer on the court and a gentleman away from the court. He was the last player anyone suspected of drug abuse, so much so that Jordan didn't believe reporters who told him of the news.

"Nah, it can't be true," Jordan said at the time.

Davis was suspended on Good Friday, just as we were discussing an insurance program for his family. Our business matters became instantly irrelevant. It was time for me to support Davis.

I went to his house after the news broke. We had a very emotional two-hour visit. I gave Davis a big hug and reminded him that we all make mistakes in life. I told him he had the opportunity to receive a fresh start by addressing his problems head on. I told him he would have to deal with the consequences of his mistake, and they would not be enjoyable. However, I promised Davis I would always support him.

Davis and I had one-on-one Bible studies for the next two years. Sometimes we met twice a week. We decided to start the Walter Davis Treatment Center and met with architects to draft our plans. Davis asked me to be his sponsor and I accepted. I even attended some Alcoholics Anonymous meetings with him, even though I have never taken drugs and didn't need to be at the meetings.

We needed to raise money for our treatment center, so I suggested we have a small dinner party at my home, followed by a fundraising dinner at a local resort on the following night. We invited former teammates and friends from the NBA and North Carolina. The guest list included Michael Jordan, Charles Barkley, James Worthy, Coach Dean Smith, Danny Ainge, John Lucas, Phil Ford, Mitch Kupchak, Sean Elliott, Charlie Scott, and Al Wood. They all came, and Jordan offered his full support.

We held fundraising dinners in successive years. In 1987, Lucas was our guest speaker—and an impactful voice. After his own bouts with drugs and alcohol, Lucas found sobriety and was dedicated to helping others do the same. Kyle Rote Jr. spoke the following year.

Along the way, we changed our minds about building the center. Instead, we took the money from our fundraisers and deposited the funds with the Arizona Community Foundation. Under the direction of Davis, the money was then distributed to drug treatment centers in Arizona.

Years later, I was able to help another former Tar Heel great.

I became friends with David Thompson after his stellar career ended. Thompson led North Carolina to the 1984 NCAA title. His nickname was Skywalker, a tribute to his amazing jumping ability. Jordan once told me that Thompson could leap higher than him, and that's saying something.

Thompson's career was also marred by drugs and alcohol, and that downward spiral continued after his playing days.

In 1990, Thompson spent a couple of nights at our home in Phoenix. During his visit, I noticed he was drinking a beer. I questioned him about his drinking because I knew he had a substance abuse problem. To my surprise, he really opened up with me.

He said he had previously tried professional treatment, but only for a day or two because he always put basketball first. Thompson felt tremendous pressure from his employers because the teams he played for wanted him on the court and not in treatment. Consequently, he had never given himself a real opportunity to beat his addictions.

I suggested that he return to treatment, and Thompson was very receptive.

At the time, Thompson was doing community service work for the Charlotte Hornets. So I called the team's owner, George Shinn. With Thompson's permission, I told Shinn about our conversation. I told him that Thompson desperately wanted to change his life. He desperately wanted to get back together with his wife, Cathy, and his two daughters, Erica and Brooke. His marriage had failed due to substance abuse.

My goal was to get Thompson into the NBA's drug rehabilitation program. I informed Shinn that I would fly Thompson to Charlotte on my own dime if we could meet with him and the team's general manager, Carl Scheer. And several days later, Thompson poured out his soul to all of us over lunch.

We were in tears as he shared his story. I told Shinn and Scheer about my history with Walter Davis, who had asked me to sponsor him during his recovery at the NBA program in Van Nuys, California. I shared how I would periodically visit the former NBA great, and I let them know that I would be happy to do the same for Thompson.

Even though I had encouraged David to seek treatment, the choice had to be coming from his heart. There was no doubt, he was ready. After our meeting, we flew to California. I checked Thompson into rehab, where he stayed for nearly two months.

When Thompson's wife saw the changes in him, they put their marriage back together. He became a Christian and devotes much of his time today working with young kids. Former NBA great Bobby Jones was an important influence for Thompson in Charlotte, North Carolina. Thompson was inducted into the Naismith Memorial Basketball Hall of Fame in 1996.

I have seen firsthand how drugs and alcohol abuse can tear apart lives and families. Unfortunately, these stories don't always come with happy endings.

Once I was attending the Clive Davis party, which is a real hard ticket. It is the party of all parties before the Grammys, and you can attend by special invitation only.

I had become friends with the legendary Clive Davis when we honored him at Celebrity Fight Night. Ever since, I've always been invited and I always attend his party. It includes all the Grammy stars in a small, intimate setting inside the Beverly Hilton hotel.

The same year we honored Davis, I became briefly acquainted with Whitney Houston. I knew she was raised with a Christian background. I knew she sung in her church. Like many people, I was aware of the struggles she had with addiction.

I also knew she would be at the Clive Davis party in 2012, and I scheduled a meeting with her beforehand. We were going to meet at 4:00 p.m., after she came off rehearsal. My only purpose for the meeting was to pray with her and encourage her. I was also going to give her a small wooden cross that I knew she would accept. I hoped that cross would be a powerful reminder for Whitney of the sacrifice Christ made for us on the cross, maybe even inspire her to conquer her demons.

I had already checked into my room on the third floor. Whitney's room was one floor above me. I was preparing for our meeting when I received a phone call from one of her friends.

"Jimmy, Whitney is dead," he said.

"What?" I asked in disbelief.

"I can't talk, but Whitney is dead," he said before hanging up.

I was stunned. Shocked. I went numb. I immediately called David Foster, who had done a lot of recordings with Whitney.

"David, I received this phone call that Whitney is dead," I said.

"Yes, it's true," Foster replied and hung up.

I turned on the television in my hotel room. It was all over CNN. I looked out my window and saw fire trucks, ambulances, and police cars in the driveway of the Beverly Hilton. And that's when I realized that Whitney must be dead.

I went downstairs to the lobby. People were crying. My heart was racing. And about twenty minutes later, I saw her friend. I told him I was just about to pray with Whitney, and that I was just about give her this wooden cross.

"Jimmy, let me take that cross," he said. "I'm going up to her room and I'm going to lay it on her."

We later learned that she drowned in her bathtub. But at the time, we had no idea how to proceed. Everyone wondered if Clive Davis was still going to host his famous party after such a tragedy.

About ninety minutes later, they announced the event would still take place. Everyone agreed that Whitney Houston would have wanted the party to go on.

It was the most sober, sad party I've ever attended in my life.

CHAPTER 16

FAITH

My Most Important Relationship

I WILL TALK OPENLY ABOUT MY FAITH IN THIS CHAPTER. MY relationship with Jesus Christ and my strong desire to live a Christian life has been the driving force in my life. I have been transparent throughout the course of this book, sharing many ups and downs along the way. I would be remiss if I didn't share how my faith has served me over the course of my life.

It may also be important to you. I sincerely believe you will benefit from hearing my story. However, if this subject disinterests you, I do not want to force my faith on anyone. If you want to skip this chapter entirely, I will not be offended.

My priorities in life are faith, family, friends, and business. I believe these priorities can help everyone lead and live a better life. That said, it took me a while to see the light and come to a deep faith.

From elementary school through high school, I went to church. But I looked at Christianity as a club. At age fifteen, I attended a camp in Colorado sponsored by Young Life, where I prayed to receive Jesus as my Lord and Savior.

Truth is, I went to this camp because I heard they had a basket-ball court and a lot of pretty girls would be attending. Count me in.

I never had a drink in high school, but I made up for it in college. I looked good from the outside. I was often the life of the party, if not the party itself. But I was empty inside.

I was often seen at the Red Dog discotheque in Scottsdale. I was only nineteen, maybe twenty, but I was armed with a fake I.D. that worked like a charm. My favorite drink in college was a "CC7," short for Canadian Club whisky and 7UP. Over time, I became more sophisticated and started drinking scotch, preferably Chivas Regal.

Things changed shortly after Nancy and I were married in 1967. Nancy started working on me, and we regularly attended church services. Three years into our marriage, our first child was born hydrocephalic. Sadly, our daughter Cynthia Faye only lived approx-imately five days.

Today my faith is extremely important. My mentor, Larry Wright, introduced me to Bible study many years ago. He told me the famous Christian sport is judging other people. We should never judge people for two reasons: number one, because we are not worthy and number two, because we never have enough information.

He was right.

Today I need the nourishment and fortification that comes with reading the Bible every day. Author Zig Ziglar once said, "I read the newspaper every day and the Bible every day, and that way I know what both sides are up to." Wright would tell me if I didn't feel like reading the Bible, read it anyway.

I have known the Lord for many years. However, at my advanced age, I am just beginning my intimacy with the Lord. Today I am leaning on the Lord more than ever. I know nothing goes unnoticed by God.

We need to realize the number one source of stress in today's world is not work. It's worry. Work doesn't keep us up at night. Worry does. In the Bible, God makes it clear what he thinks about worry.

Philippians 4:6-7 says, "Don't worry about anything; instead, pray about everything; tell God your needs, and don't forget to thank him for his answers. If you do this, you will experience God's peace ..." (TLB). When we worry about something, we are telling God that we don't think He can handle it. Worrying exaggerates the problem. Worrying is unproductive. Worrying is unhelpful. The only thing worrying changes is you and I, and it makes us miserable.

Moses gave us the Ten Commandments in the book of Exodus.

Sadly, too many people look at the Ten Commandments as the Ten Suggestions, and they just do whatever they please.

Corinthians 13:13 says among faith, hope, and love, the greatest of these gifts is love.

This is also what Muhammad Ali told me for years. He would say, "The greatest religion in the world is the religion of love."

Over a twenty-year period, I spent many hours doing charity work with Ali. I never saw him refuse an autograph or refuse to have his picture taken with one of his fans. I never heard Ali say a bad word about anyone. Why?

The Champ practiced what he preached. He practiced love with all people.

Martin Luther King Jr. said, "I have decided to stick with love ... Hate is too great of a burden to bear."

Mother Teresa said, "If we judge people, we don't have time to love them."

Rabbi Amanda Greene said, "Love makes us strong. Love gives us courage to act. Love gives us hope."

Author Ken Blanchard once asked historian Peter Drucker if he was a Christian. Drucker answered, "Yes, I am a Christian." Blanchard asked Drucker, "Why are you a Christian?" Drucker said, "I've checked out all the other options. There is no better deal! After all, what other religion offers grace? Grace deals with our self-esteem and our self-worth, and the only way we can receive God's forgiveness is through His grace."

All we need to know is God loves us unconditionally, which is the definition of grace.

People are given freedom to make their own choices. Religion is no different. But while trends change and popular opinions change, the Word of God does not. The Word of God never changes.

There are two important components of belief. They are love and doctrine. I believe in the Old Testament and the New Testament. However, should I not agree with someone else's religious beliefs, I always want to show that person love and respect, and I never want to be judgmental.

Author John Maxwell said every person has a "Why?" along with the ability to find it. I believe it's important to ask questions. The late Larry King asked me "Why?" many times during our conversations about the Bible. By the way, who would know better than the king of talk show hosts when it comes to asking questions than Larry King?

My last visit with Larry was when we were in Florence, Italy. From time to time, Larry had publicly commented on CNN that he did not know if he believed in God or not. Before our visit in Italy, I asked Larry if I had his permission to talk about what the Bible says about our salvation. Larry replied, "Yes, of course . . . No problem." Incidentally Larry was always firing questions at me. He liked to talk about Jesus and, personally, I believe today Larry is at home with the Lord.

Becky Radant was Larry King's executive assistant for many years, and she told me the following two days after King's death,

"I want you to know, Jimmy, that it has always meant the world to me that you talked with Larry about the Bible. Thank you for your prayers and for being a good friend."

I also know religion can turn people off very quickly. NFL Hall of Fame quarterback Kurt Warner learned from experience the consequences of coming on too strong. He learned how to love Jesus and share His teachings in mainstream, unobtrusive ways.

For proof, Lonnie Ali is of Muslim faith. She told me she really admired Kurt Warner for not wearing his religion on his sleeve.

When Warner was receiving his Humanitarian Award from Muhammad Ali at Celebrity Fight Night sometime back, Lonnie told an audience of 1,200 people that Kurt "is an excellent example to all of us with his faith since he does such a good job with his family and in our community."

In other words, well done is better than well said.

I have also learned the hard way. Once I was in the back of a cab on my way to the airport for a flight home from Washington, D.C. The cab driver and I were having a nice conversation. Until I mentioned Jesus.

The cab driver turned around and screamed at me: "If you ever mention the name, Jesus, again I am going to kick you out of this cab!" he said.

I stopped the conversation. Sadly, we can mention other religious leaders by name. But mention Jesus and it can quickly irritate some people.

Around 1970, I was visiting with Reggie Jackson during spring training in Florida when he was playing for the Yankees. We were driving around in his Rolls-Royce and I began talking about Jesus. I came on too heavy, and I could tell Reggie was uncomfortable. But I was a relative newcomer in my faith; today, my goal is to share my faith when appropriate, hopefully in a gentle and respectful way.

Religion turns many people off. I don't care to be known as being religious; however, I am not ashamed to say that I have a personal relationship with Jesus. In Romans 1:16 the apostle Paul implores us to not be ashamed of the gospel.

Today, the world feels broken by anger, hatred, riots, racial division, and political discord. To combat all of the negativity around us, Jerry Colangelo, once the majority owner of the Phoenix Suns and Arizona Diamondbacks, and I began filming faith-based virtual broadcasts. During an episode we called "Living in Difficult Times," we featured former NFL head coach Tony Dungy, who lost his son, James, to suicide. During the broadcast, we had Michael W. Smith sing "Waymaker."

In our broadcast on "Overcoming Today's Challenges," we featured Phoenix Suns head coach Monty Williams, who also endured personal tragedy. Williams lost his wife, Ingrid, following a car accident with a woman who was on drugs. We dialed in David Foster and his wife Katherine to sing "The Prayer."

In our Christmas episode, "Following a Star and Finding a Stable," we featured author John Maxwell. Our musical selection for that broadcast was Andrea Bocelli, who sang "Silent Night" from his piano in Italy. Colangelo also spoke on "The Importance of Faith," and Reba McEntire sang "Back to God" and she shared the importance of her faith.

Pastor Rick Warren, author of *The Purpose Driven Life*, spoke during our episode on "Why Prayer Is Important." In that episode, we had Bocelli, Foster, and Pia Toscano sing "The Prayer."

If you ask most people what they want to achieve in life, the majority will respond by saying, "I want to be happy." Whether a person is wealthy or homeless, this is a common answer. People want to be happy. I have found the best path to happiness is by spreading it to others. The answer to being happy is to find a way to make other people happy.

I believe one of the best scriptures about happiness says (and I paraphrase), "To much is given, much is expected" (Luke 12:48). It's all about giving.

Many people who are hospitalized today deal with depression issues. We are all human and we all battle disappointments and discouragement. Perhaps the next time we are down in the dumps, we should make a list of fifty things for which we are thankful. That's called gratitude. I believe it's important to list the smallest things we take for granted in life. I know this helps me when I have my personal pity party or I become too self-centered, when I focus too much on my needs and not on others who are living in a worse situation.

Author C.S. Lewis said, "True humility is not thinking less of yourself. It is thinking of yourself less."

Gratitude is not only important. It can get your mind in the right place, and it can help you heal.

I have found that the Bible gives us all the answers we need. The Bible stands for Basic Instructions Before Leaving Earth. To grow as a Christian, I need to pray every day. Prayer is so important. I also believe in microwave prayers, which are quick and right to the point. For instance, when temptation strikes and you don't have time for a long conversation with God, that's when you need a microwave prayer.

Famed evangelist Billy Graham said if he could change two things in his life, it would be to spend more time with his family and more time in prayer. He also said, "All my prayers were answered except when I was playing golf."

On a related note, comedian Billy Crystal told me his golf game is like Israel: they both have problems in the sand.

Prayer is simply having a conversation with God. However, I sometimes tend to lose my focus while praying. I struggle with concentration. My thoughts begin to scatter, and I struggle with what to say and how to say it. I know I have an inventory of needs.

And sometimes, I fail to pray where I sometimes have secret wounds, which are hidden in places only the Lord can heal.

Life is not easy. Discouragement happens to everyone, which is why prayer is so important. Every person I have ever met is going through a challenge.

I also know my day is better when I talk to God first. I can enter prayer in a certain mood and come out in another mood altogether. I believe seven days without prayer makes a person weak. Someone once told me, "Pray and believe and expect to receive; pray and doubt and expect to be left out." Corrie ten Boom once asked, "Is prayer your steering wheel or your spare tire?"

God answers every prayer with a yes, no, or wait. If God answered every prayer immediately, you would begin to think He was a vending machine. Put in a prayer and pull out whatever you need.

The Bible is the most positive book I have ever read. It explains life better than any other book. Charles Spurgeon said, "The Bible is not to increase our knowledge but to change our life."

Billy Graham read five psalms every day, which taught him how to get along with God. He read one chapter of Proverbs every day, which taught him how to get along with people. You don't get blessed by reading the Bible. You get blessed by applying the Bible. God gave us the Bible so we can know Him.

Oswald Chambers said, "If we understood what happens when we read the Bible, we would read it more often."

Unfortunately, Bibles are not allowed in many schools, but they are encouraged in prisons. Perhaps if kids were allowed to read the Bible in school, they would not end up in prison.

Comedian Jay Leno said, "With hurricanes, tornados, fires out of control, flooding, terrorist attacks, are you sure this is a good time to take God out of the Pledge of Allegiance?" I am encouraged when celebrities in the entertainment world speak up for God.

The entire New Testament can be summed up in nine words. Jesus said, "If you love me, you will keep my commandments" (John 14:15 ESV).

The opposite of wealth accumulation is generosity of your time, talent, and treasure. The opposite of recognition is service to others. When we focus our lives on creating significance, we will be amazed at how much success will come our way.

Significance is all about what we can do for others. I believe self-ishness and self-centeredness are at the root of virtually every problem, personally and globally. And whether we want to admit it or not, it's a problem all of us have. Jesus always puts the needs of others first.

John Maxwell often asks people, "What's your story?" He understands that we all have a bit of humor in our stories, as well as some drama. We all have our ups and downs, our wins and losses. We want our stories to be of significance.

I feel greatness is reserved for those with a servant's heart and humility.

I have been leading a Bible study group for many years. I am not a theologian. In many ways, I don't even feel qualified to lead a Bible study since I still struggle in so many areas of my own life. I know I am flawed. I also believe if God can use someone like me to lead a Bible study, he can use anyone. I am still working every day on my PhD degree…Patience, Humility, and Discipline. There is no tuition in the school of experience. We need to view adversity as a learning experience.

The flesh and the spirit are always in conflict. Even after years of leading Bible study, there is still a macho side of me where I want things my way. It's a desire for control. I like what NFL superstar Russell Wilson said when receiving the Muhammad Ali Humanitarian award at Celebrity Fight Night. He quoted John 3:30: "He must increase, but I must decrease" (ESV).

Author Rick Warren said, "If God used perfect people, nothing would get done. God will use anybody if we are available." It's not our ability as much as our availability.

Our Bible study is not church-sponsored. We are not a club. We are not an organization. There are no dues to pay and nothing required to join. When I lead Bible study, I make it a point not to discuss psychology or my philosophy on life. Instead, we are going to study the scriptures. If we abide in the Word, we will know the Truth, and the Truth will set you free (John 8:31).

I hold a monthly event with my four grandsons. We call it Papa's Steak Night. It's fifteen minutes of Bible study followed by fifteen minutes on the subject of hospitality. Then I cook a steak dinner. We read chapters out of Rick Warren's book *The Purpose Driven Life*. The kids ask me great questions, and it's important that I make the Bible study fun.

On the subject of hospitality, I stress upon my grandchildren the importance of little things like opening a door for a woman, how to say "Yes, sir" and "Yes, ma'am," how to look a person in the eye and deliver a firm handshake, and how to say the words, "Nice meeting you." Hospitality classes are not taught in school.

I have been doing this for over a decade. When the kids were younger, they just giggled and devoured the steak. Now they are really paying attention. They understand the importance of good manners and the power of saying "thank you" and "you're welcome."

My grandson Justin said to me at age eight, "Papa, you are not very good with computers."

"I know that, Justin," I said. "But don't ever forget, Papa taught you how to use a spoon."

I have learned from experience that you have to be quick on your feet with these young kids.

God grows us one step at a time. Most of us are slow learners. I know I often have to relearn a lesson several times. Growth for me can be painful. But God is more interested in our growth than our comfort.

I know after many years of marriage that I can be a better husband, more patient and kind. I know I can be a better dad and papa. It really all comes down to our priorities and our attitude. I know that I can become too self-centered instead of being Christ-centered.

Over the years, my wife and I have hosted over fifteen dinner parties for friends who shared their testimony about their Christian faith. Once we featured Hall of Fame basketball star Pete Maravich. He was introduced by former Suns head coach Paul Westphal. And later that evening, we had Glen Campbell sing and play his acoustic guitar on our patio, in the company of around 150 people.

"Pistol" Pete was a basketball legend, with skills far ahead of his time. He struggled with his own demons. He shared the misery of his life before he found the Lord.

Maravich would walk into a bar and tell everyone, "Hey, boys, the drinks are on Pistol!" He would have one drink and it was all downhill from there. He shared how he once started talking to a girl at a bar, and her boyfriend showed up. The boyfriend didn't like it one bit. Pete found himself in the parking lot of that bar with a gun barrel down his throat. The man said, "Pistol Pete, you are finished!" By the grace of God, that man never pulled the trigger.

Maravich quoted the scripture many times. "Let your light shine before people in such a way that they may see your good works, and glorify your Father who is in Heaven" (Matthew 5:16 NASB). In other words, it's all about our integrity and our character. Warren Buffett said, "It takes twenty years to build a reputation and five minutes to destroy it."

Elgin Baylor was also one of the best basketball players in history, and he and I were pallbearers at Maravich's funeral. Westphal and

Campbell have also passed, and I'm sure they are enjoying quite a reunion in Heaven.

I love what Pastor Rick Warren once said about Heaven: "You will not be in Heaven two seconds before you cry out, 'Why did I place so much importance on things that were so temporary?'"

I try not to flaunt the awards I have won in my life. You won't see them on the walls in my office or in my home. The exception is the award I received in 2003 from the American Jewish Committee. It is their National Human Relations award. The gift is a three-foot statue of the prophet Isaiah, and it is very meaningful to me because he was the greatest prophet of them all. The prophet Isaiah means a lot to a Christian, just like my rabbi friend in Los Angeles who couldn't wait to tell me he had written my name on a piece of paper and placed it in the Wailing Wall in Jerusalem, Israel.

I love Israel. After Billy Crystal entertained our guests at a Celebrity Fight Night, we made a donation to Hebrew University in Jerusalem for $500,000 to honor him.

Without the Jews, we would have no Bible, Jesus, or the Ten Commandments. God promises to bless those who bless Israel and curse those who curse Israel. I love reading about the Jewish Prophet Isaiah, who was inspired by God when he wrote (and I paraphrase):

Isaiah 40:29: God gives power to you when you are tired and worn out.

Isaiah 41:10: God is always with you. Fear not, for I am with you. I will strengthen you with your problems and I will help you.

Isaiah 43:2: No matter what you may be facing, God is right there with you.

Isaiah 55:8: My ways are higher than your ways and my thoughts are higher than your thoughts.

Isaiah 61:3: God can change your time of depression into joy.

I also believe in forming your own accountability group. This group of people should really care about you without any strings attached. These are people who can guide you in the right direction when you need good advice.

I call my accountability group The Lineup. They are:

1. My wife, Nancy, on all issues.
2. Jamie Rasmussen, on the Bible.
3. Rick Warren and the late Foster Friess, on finding your purpose in life.
4. Jerry Colangelo, Lee and Nancy Hanley, Glenn Stearns, Mike Ingram, and Jerry Moyes on the importance of family.
5. John Maxwell and Ken Blanchard, on understanding success vs. significance.
6. Harlan Schneider and Anne Ross, on managing your finances.
7. John Langbein, Dan Andriano, Harvey Mackay, Dave Cavan, Michael W. Smith, and Tom Shine, on relationships.
8. Rod Bentley, Grant Sardachuk, Mark Buckley, Jennifer Evans, Mac Magruder, Jim Dennis, and Dr. Michel Sucher on helping those with addiction.
9. Steve Zabilski and Jerry Castro, on working with the homeless.
10. The late Bruce Halle, on business integrity and leadership.

When I have serious questions, these are the people I lean on.

I think everybody has blind spots. Other people can easily see what is wrong in our lives, things that may be out of order. They can see things better than we can because we all have blind spots.

These were among the last words from Steve Jobs before his death:

Apart from my work, I have little joy. At this time, lying on the hospital bed and remembering all my life, I realize all the accolades and riches of which I was so proud have become insignificant with my imminent death approaching. I know death is looming over me. Only now do I understand that once you have accumulated enough money for the rest of your life, you have to pursue other objectives that are not related to wealth. It should be something more important. For example: stories of love, art, dreams of my childhood. Stop pursuing wealth. It can only make a person into a twisted being, just like me. I cannot take my fame with me. But love can travel thousands of miles and so life has no limits.

God isn't impressed with our status. He is impressed with our service. Mother Teresa said, "God has not called me to be successful. He has called me to be faithful." Faith is like a muscle. You need to exercise it for it to grow.

I recently met a homeless man named Fuzzy.

I saw Fuzzy walking near an intersection and motioned for him to meet me about 200 feet away, in a Safeway parking lot. After visiting for a few minutes, I asked him a question: "Fuzzy, if your heart stopped beating today and you dropped dead, are you 100 percent sure you would be in Heaven?"

He didn't hesitate.

"I am 100 percent sure because of Good Old Dad," he said.

I was confused.

"What does 'Good Old Dad' mean?" I said.

"It means God. G-O-D. Good Old Dad."

Fuzzy told me what I already knew. He told me if I tell people about God, it will turn them off. So Fuzzy refers to Him as Good Old Dad, and then he can talk to people about God.

I loved his answer. More importantly, God knows Fuzzy's heart.

As I bring this book to a close, I'd like to finish our journey with two very important scriptures. The first is from the Old Testament: "'For I know the plans I have for you,' declares the Lord. 'Plans to prosper you and not to harm you, plans to give you hope and a future.'" (Jeremiah 29:11 NIV).

The second is from the New Testament: "For God so loved the world that He gave His one and only Son, that whoever believes in Him shall not perish but have eternal life" (John 3:16 NIV).

At the end of our lives, God will give us a final test. He won't ask us if we achieved straight As in school. He won't care how well we did in our careers. He won't ask to see our bank account balance.

Instead, He will ask the following:

Did you get to know me? Did you build a relationship with my Son who I sent to Earth to die on the cross for you?

I have built and nurtured a lot of relationships in my life, and I have learned from them all. But the most important relationship in my life has been the one with my heavenly Father. Knowing God is the most important thing. Not knowing *about* Him. But knowing Him personally.

That is how you build a life that matters.

A NOTE FROM THE AUTHOR

REALIZING THERE IS NO GREATER LOSS OR PAIN IN LIFE FOR A parent than losing their child, the purpose of this book is in memory of my son, Scott, who told me on December 12, 2019, just three days before he accidentally overdosed, "Dad, I want to build a sober living home to help other people suffering from the same disease that I have with addiction."

I said, "Scott, your dad will help you build this sober living home."

One hundred percent of the profits from this book will go to develop sober living homes in Phoenix and Scottsdale. Plus, this book will be distributed complimentary from gifts from foundations and individuals who want to help thousands of men and women to make the right choices who are currently in rehabilitation centers, sober living homes, schools, and other locations throughout the United States.

I believe the biggest problem in America today is drugs attacking numerous families. The answer to this growing problem is to say no to drugs.

Our family wants to help others suffering from this terrible disease.

ACKNOWLEDGMENTS

THANK YOU TO DAN BICKLEY AND GREG BOECK, WHO SAT with me for hours and helped tell my story.

Thank you to John Maxwell and Harvey Mackay, who helped with this book's structure and purpose.

Thank you to my publisher, Jonathan Merkh of Forefront Books, along with Lauren Ward and my editor Jen Gingerich.

Thank you to Megan and Emma, my executive assistants who help me remain focused every day, and who go to great lengths to make sure I don't leave my iPhone at the office.

NOTES

1 Jaime Rosenberg, "5 Updates on Trends in Drug Overdose Deaths in the United States," AJMC, August 2, 2019, https://www.ajmc.com/view/5-up-dates-on-trends-in-drug-overdose-death--in-the-united-states.

2 "Health Consequences of Drug Misuse: Death," National Institute on Drug Abuse, https://www.drugabuse.gov/drug-topics/health-consequenc-es-drug-misuse/death.

3 "Provisional Drug Overdose Death Counts," Centers for Disease Control and Prevention, https://www.cdc.gov/nchs/nvss/vsrr/drug-overdose-data.htm.

4 "2018 National Drug Threat Assessment," U.S. Department of Justice Drug Enforcement Administration, https://www.dea.gov/sites/default/files/2018-11/DIR-032-18%202018%20NDTA%20final%20low%20reso-lution.pdf.

5 Skylar Kenney, "COVID-19 Pandemic Results in Increased Substance Use Among Regular Drug Users," *Pharmacy Times*, April 27, 2021, https://www.pharmacytimes.com/view/covid-19-pandemic-results-in-increased-substance-use-among-regular-drug-users.

6 Francis Collins, "After Opioid Overdose, Most Young People Aren't Getting Addiction Treatment," NIH Director's Blog, January 28, 2020, https://directorsblog.nih.gov/2020/01/28/after-opioid-over-dose-most-young-people-arent-getting-addiction-treatment/.

7 Ibid.

8 Ibid.

INDEX

(Page numbers in *italics* refer to photos or captions.)